# 100
# REAL ESTATE
## MARKETING IDEAS

**A Playbook For Agents:** Proven Strategies &
Tips for Realtors To Generate More Leads,
Build A Better Brand And Win More Clients

## Nick Tsai &
### The Soldouthouses.com's Team

100 Real Estate Marketing Ideas by Nick Tsai

Published by Wishstone Trading Limited

Https://soldouthouses.com

Copyright © 2022 Nick Tsai

# BONUSES

Thanks for getting this book; here are some resources to help you bring your real estate career to the next level.

**Bonus 1- A 14 Days Free Trial Of Our Membership**

You can also join our pro membership to get access to over 1700+ real estate marketing tools & templates for only a few bucks a day.

Go to https://soldouthouses.com/pro/ to try it for free.

**Bonus 2- The Ultimate Real Estate Marketing Checklist**

This checklist features 86 marketing tips to generate more leads online & offline.

Download your free checklist at
https://soldouthouses.com/checklist

# TABLE OF CONTENT

# INTRODUCTION

Welcome to 100 Real Estate Marketing Ideas. Our team has compiled an exhaustive list of proven strategies for realtors and agents to generate more leads. Who doesn't want more leads?

This book is designed to provide Real Estate professionals with a comprehensive guide to generating leads and boosting sales through various marketing strategies. This guide is organized into several chapters, each chapter covering different aspects of real estate marketing.

- In the "Social Media Marketing Ideas" chapter, you will learn about different ways to use social media to promote your listings and generate leads.
- The "Marketing with Your Website" chapter will cover strategies for building and optimizing your website to attract more clients.
- The "Content Marketing Ideas" chapter will teach you how to use content marketing to generate leads.
- The "Offline Marketing Ideas" chapter will cover offline strategies such as open houses and networking events.
- The "Creative Online Marketing Ideas" chapter will cover unique and creative ways to generate leads online.

- The "Unique and Creative Ideas for Real Estate Marketing" chapter will cover even more unique and creative ideas to boost your sales.
- The "Real Estate Advertising Strategies Using Online Tools" chapter will show you how to use online tools to create effective and efficient advertising campaigns.

To get the most out of this book, it's important to read it thoroughly and take notes of the tips and strategies that apply to your business. It's also recommended to pick a few strategies and focus on implementing them before moving on to the next one. The book is full of actionable tips and strategies you can implement today.

As you read this informative book, you will gain valuable information and inspiration to help you generate more leads and boost your sales. You can succeed in the competitive real estate world with the right marketing strategies.

# ABOUT ME

Who Am I?

Hi, my name is Nick Tsai. I'm a digital marketing expert with over a decade of experience. Once a real estate agent myself, I understand the struggles of generating leads and closing sales in this competitive industry.

When I started as a realtor, I followed the traditional advice of the industry. But despite my best efforts, I still didn't get the results I was looking for. I was frustrated, exhausted, and began to lose hope.

But then something changed. I received a phone call from a stranger asking me to help him sell a house. I had never called or mailed him and didn't even know who he was. But he had found my website - an ugly blog that I had started using as a personal notebook to document everything I was learning about real estate. Surprisingly, it had become my local area's #1 ranking real estate blog.

From there, I started getting more and more calls and requests for help. People were reaching out to me, asking for advice and asking to be taken on as clients. I realized it was far easier to attract clients than to chase them. By harnessing the power of the internet, I could reach people ready to buy and position myself as the expert they needed.

That's when I decided to dive deep into digital marketing and learn everything I could about how to generate leads online. I studied countless books, attended seminars, and learned from the best experts in the field. I decided to create SoldOutHouses.com as a resource for other real estate professionals who want to get results with digital marketing. I encourage you to reach out and see how we can help you.

We hope you gain a lot of insight from this comprehensive guide.

Talk soon,

Nick

To generate more leads and close sales, visit https://SoldOutHouses.com.

Discover countless real estate marketing tools and templates.

Follow our YouTube channel at https://youtube.com/@soldouthouses.

# SOCIAL MEDIA MARKETING IDEAS

## WHY SOCIAL MEDIA MARKETING

Social media is a powerful tool for real estate agents looking to generate leads. It allows you to connect with potential clients, promote your listings, and build your brand. By creating a strong online presence, you can reach a wider audience and increase your chances of finding the right buyers or sellers for your properties.

Did you know nearly 75% of the world's population aged 13 and older use social media weekly, and over 93% of regular internet users log into social media semi-regularly?

One of the biggest benefits of using social media for real estate lead generation is the ability to target specific demographics. For example, suppose your ideal client is a young family looking for a starter home. You should target your advertising to reach that audience. Using social media platforms like Facebook, Twitter, and Instagram, you can create ads targeting specific groups based on their interests, demographics, and location.

Another way to use social media for lead generation is to share your listings on your social media accounts. You can post pictures and information about your properties, as well as open house dates and times. These are great ways to attract potential buyers and sellers and keep current clients informed about your latest listings.

In this first chapter, I will share different ideas for using social media to generate online leads.

If you need our done-for-you social media posts, you can also go to https://soldouthouses.com/365doneforyoucontent to grab your copy for a discount.

## 1. FACEBOOK MARKETING

Generating leads from Facebook is an effective way for realtors to connect with potential clients and grow their businesses. With over 2 billion monthly active users, Facebook offers an audience for realtors to market their services.

Here are a few strategies that realtors can use to generate leads from Facebook:

1.  **Create a Business Page:** The first step to generating leads on Facebook is to create a business page. Your business page is where you share information about your business, including your services, testimonials, and listings. By having a business page, you can run targeted ads to specific demographics, interests, and behaviors. Thus, making this the ideal place to advertise.

2.  **Optimize Your Business Page:** Once you have a business page, optimize it for lead generation. It is important to include a call-to-action button, such as "Contact Us" or "Learn More," on your page. You should also include your contact information, cell and office numbers, and email addresses so potential clients can reach you easily. In today's world, contacting you should be the easy part!

3.  **Share Valuable Content:** One of the best ways to generate leads on Facebook is to share valuable content relevant to your target audience. You can include blog posts, videos, and infographics and provide helpful tips and information about buying or selling a home. By sharing valuable content, you can establish yourself as a trusted authority in the real estate industry, which will build trust and credibility with potential clients.

4. **Run Ads:** Facebook offers a variety of advertising options for realtors to choose from, such as video ads, carousel ads, and lead generation ads. These ads are an effective way to reach a larger audience and generate leads. You can target specific demographics, interests, and behaviors, which can help you to reach the right people.

5. **Leverage Facebook Groups:** Joining and participating in Facebook groups related to real estate can be a great way to generate leads. You can join groups for buyers, sellers, and real estate professionals and use them to share your knowledge and expertise. This is also a great way to build relationships with potential clients.

6. **Use Facebook Live:** Finally, another effective way to generate leads on Facebook is to use Facebook Live. This feature allows you to broadcast live videos to your followers and stay connected with potential clients. It's easy to build relationships and answer questions. Use Facebook Live to showcase those hot properties and provide valuable tips and advice.

Facebook is a powerful tool that realtors can use to generate leads and grow their businesses.

Realtors can reach a larger audience and connect with potential clients by creating a business page.

- Optimize your page.
- Share valuable content.
- Run ads.
- Leverage Facebook groups.
- Use Facebook live.

It's important to be consistent and active on the platform and to focus on providing value to your target audience. By following these strategies, realtors can generate leads and grow their business on Facebook.

## 2. INSTAGRAM MARKETING

Instagram is a powerful platform for realtors to generate leads and grow their business. With over 1 billion monthly active users, Instagram offers a vast audience for realtors to market their

services to.

Here are a few strategies that realtors can use to generate leads from Instagram:

1. **Create a Professional Profile:** The first step to generating leads on Instagram is to create a professional profile. This includes using a clear profile picture, writing a compelling bio, and including your contact information, such as your phone number and email address. Having a professional profile can build credibility and trust with potential clients.

2. **Share Visually Appealing Content:** Instagram is a highly visual platform. Realtors should take advantage of this by sharing visually appealing content. This includes beautiful photos, videos of properties, and behind-the-scenes footage of the real estate process. You can showcase your listings and build your brand by sharing high-quality content.

3. **Use Hashtags:** Hashtags are a great way to reach a larger audience on Instagram. When you use relevant hashtags, your posts will be more likely to be seen by potential clients

searching for those specific terms. You can also create your own branded hashtags, which can help to build your brand and increase visibility.

4. **Utilize Instagram Stories:** Instagram Stories is a feature that allows you to share photos and videos that disappear after 24 hours. This feature is a great way to share behind-the-scenes footage, such as open houses, and give potential clients a glimpse into your daily life as a realtor. You can also use Instagram Stories to run polls, ask questions, and share testimonials.

5. **Leverage Instagram Live:** Instagram Live is another feature that allows you to broadcast live videos to your followers. This is a great way to connect with potential clients and build relationships. You can use Instagram Live to answer questions, showcase properties, and provide valuable tips and advice.

6. **Partner With Influencers:** Partnering with real estate or home improvement influencers can be a great way to reach a larger audience and generate leads. Influencers have a large following and can help to promote your listings and services to a larger audience.

7. **Run Ads:** Instagram also offers a variety of advertising options, such as photo ads, video ads, and carousel ads. Use these tools for advertising specific demographics, interests, and behaviors, which can help you reach the right people.

## 3. TIKTOK & OTHER SHORT VIDEO PLATFORMS

TikTok, the short-form video platform, has become one of the most popular social media platforms in recent years. With over 1 billion active users worldwide, it provides a unique opportunity for real estate professionals to generate leads and boost sales. Here are a few ways to use TikTok to achieve this goal:

1. **Create Engaging Content:** TikTok is about short, creative, and engaging videos. You can create videos that showcase properties, provide tips on buying or selling a home, or give a behind-the-scenes look at your work as a realtor. The key is to create interesting, informative, and relatable content for your target audience.

2. **Use Hashtags:** TikTok's algorithm favors videos that use popular hashtags. Using relevant hashtags, you can increase the visibility of your videos and reach a wider audience. For example, if you're creating a video about a new listing, use hashtags like #newlisting #forsale #realestate.

3. **Collaborate With Other TikTok Users:** Collaborating with other TikTok users can help increase your reach and generate leads. You can team up with local businesses, other real estate professionals, or even homeowners to create videos that showcase properties and promote your services.

4. **Utilize Instagram and Facebook:** TikTok is a great platform to showcase your personality, but it's also important to have a presence on other social media platforms. Instagram and Facebook are both options to consider.

Below we list some of the types of content that can work well on TikTok:

1. **Property Listings:** Create short videos that showcase the key features of your listings, including virtual tours of the property, walk-throughs, and highlight reels of the best features. Use hashtags that are relevant to the property and location.

2. **Tips and Advice:** Create educational and informative videos that provide tips and advice for buyers and sellers. For example, how to stage a home for sale, common mistakes to avoid when buying or selling a home, and negotiation tips. Use hashtags that are relevant to the topic and include a call to action like "DM me for more information."

3. **Testimonials:** Share testimonials from satisfied clients in short videos, showing the before and after of buying or selling a home with them.

4. **Neighborhood and Community Information:** Create videos highlighting the best aspects of the neighborhoods and communities you serve, such as local restaurants, parks, schools, and other points of interest. Use location-based hashtags and geotags to increase visibility.

5. **Personal Brand:** Create videos that showcase your personality, expertise, and approach to real estate, like "day in the life" videos, Q&A sessions, behind-the-scenes of the real estate process, and fun facts about you. Use personal hashtags and branding to increase visibility.

## 4.LINKEDIN MARKETING

LinkedIn is a professional networking platform that can be an effective tool for realtors to generate leads and grow their business. With over 722 million users worldwide, LinkedIn offers a vast audience for realtors to market their services to. Here are a few strategies that realtors can use to generate leads from LinkedIn:

1. **Create a Professional Profile:** The first step to generating LinkedIn leads is creating a professional profile. This includes using a clear profile picture, writing a compelling bio, and including your contact information, such as your phone number and email address. Having a professional profile, you can build credibility and trust with potential clients.

2. **Share Valuable Content:** LinkedIn is a great platform for sharing valuable content relevant to your target audience. This can include blog posts, videos, and infographics that provide helpful tips and information about buying or selling a home. By sharing valuable content, you can establish yourself as a trusted authority in the real estate industry, which can help to build trust and credibility with potential clients.

3. **Join and Participate in Groups:** Joining and participating in LinkedIn groups related to real estate can be a great way to generate leads. You can join groups for buyers, sellers, and real estate professionals and use them to share your knowledge and expertise and build relationships with potential clients.

4. **Leverage LinkedIn Ads:** LinkedIn offers a variety of advertising options, such as sponsored content, sponsored InMail, and display ads. These ads can target specific demographics, interests, and behaviors, which can help you reach the right people.

5. **Connect with Potential Clients:** One of the best ways to generate leads on LinkedIn is to connect with potential clients. You can send connection requests, engage in conversations, and join groups. You can establish trust and credibility by building relationships with potential clients, leading to more leads and business.

6. **Use LinkedIn Sales Navigator:** LinkedIn Sales Navigator is a tool that can help realtors find and connect with potential clients. It allows you to create lists of leads, track their activity, and get insights into their company and industry.

## 5. TWITTER

Twitter is a powerful tool that can help realtors reach a wider audience and connect with potential clients. By creating a professional Twitter account and regularly posting updates, realtors can showcase their listings, share industry news, and offer valuable tips and advice to their followers.

One of the key benefits of Twitter is that it allows realtors to connect with a large community of people who are interested in real estate. By following industry leaders and other realtors, you can stay up-to-date on the latest trends and best practices in the industry and share this information with your followers. Additionally, using relevant hashtags and keywords can increase your visibility and reach potential clients searching for information about buying or selling a home.

Another advantage of Twitter is that it allows realtors to build relationships with potential clients. By responding to tweets, direct messages, and mentions, you can show that you are responsive and engaged with your followers. Additionally, by hosting Twitter chats or Q&A sessions, you can provide valuable information and demonstrate your expertise in the industry.

Twitter can also be used to promote your listings and open houses. By sharing high-quality photos and videos of your properties, you can give potential buyers a better sense of what the home is like and entice them to schedule a showing. Additionally, you can attract more people to your properties by tweeting about upcoming open houses or virtual tours.

In addition to these strategies, realtors can also use Twitter to drive traffic to their website and other online platforms, such as their blog, Instagram, and Facebook. You can direct your followers to additional information about your listings and services by including links in your tweets.

Twitter is a powerful social media platform realtors can use to connect with potential clients, promote their listings, and build their brands. Realtors can increase their visibility and reach a wider audience by following industry leaders, using relevant hashtags, and regularly posting updates.

By engaging with their followers and providing valuable information, realtors can build relationships with potential clients and establish themselves as experts in the industry.

## 6. USE VIDEOS TO YOUR ADVANTAGE

Videos are a powerful tool for real estate agents looking to market their listings and attract new leads. They provide a unique and engaging way to showcase properties and can be a great way to differentiate your business from the competition.

One strategy to use videos in your real estate marketing efforts is creating property walkthrough videos. These videos can be used to give potential buyers and sellers a virtual tour of a property. You are allowing them to see all the features and benefits of the property without having to schedule a viewing. This can save time for both buyers and realtors and can also generate more Interest in a property.

Another strategy is to create neighborhood and community videos. Use these videos to highlight the benefits of living in a particular area and showcase the local events, businesses, and attractions. These videos can help potential buyers to see the appeal of the neighborhood and community and make them more likely to consider purchasing a property in the area.

You can also create videos that highlight the unique features of a property. For example, you can create a video showcasing the property's backyard, which is perfect for hosting summer barbecues. Or create a video highlighting the property's open floor plan, which is perfect for entertaining.

You can also create videos that show the behind-the-scenes of your business, such as videos of your team or videos of you working with clients. Helping make it more relatable to potential buyers and sellers.

## 7. TAKE ADVANTAGE OF INFOGRAPHICS

Infographics are a powerful marketing tool for realtors. Not only do they grab attention, but they also make it easy for potential clients to understand complex information quickly.

Here are some ways realtors can use infographics in their marketing:

1. **Showcase Neighborhood Information:** Create an infographic that showcases important information about the neighborhoods you specialize in, such as median home prices, crime rates, and school ratings.

2. **Compare Rent vs. Buy:** Create an infographic that compares the costs of renting a home versus buying a home. Helping potential buyers understand home ownership's long-term financial benefits.

3. **Highlight the Home-buying Process:** Create an infographic highlighting the steps involved in buying a home. This can help potential buyers understand the process and feel more comfortable purchasing.

4. **Share Testimonials:** Create an infographic showcasing satisfied clients' testimonials. Testimonials help potential clients understand your level of expertise and the quality of service you provide.

5. **Share Real Estate Market Trends:** Create an infographic that highlights current real estate market trends. We can help potential buyers and sellers understand the current market conditions and make more informed decisions.

By using infographics in your marketing, you can make complex information easy to understand and grab the attention of potential clients. Infographics can be shared on social media, included in email marketing campaigns, and even printed out and used as part of an open house or listing presentation.

Infographics are a powerful marketing tool for realtors. They can help potential clients understand complex information quickly, grab attention, and help them make more informed decisions. You can use infographics to showcase neighborhood information. Compare rent vs. buy, highlight the home-buying process, share testimonials, and share real estate market trends.

Using infographics in your marketing can stand out from the competition and make a lasting impression on potential clients.

If you want to save time & money on creating those infographics, You can get our done-for-you infographic package at https://soldouthouses.com/infographics.

## 8. USE THE RIGHT TOOL TO MANAGE YOUR SOCIAL MEDIA

Using software to manage multiple social media accounts can be an effective way for realtors to generate leads and grow their businesses. Here are a few strategies for using software to manage multiple social media accounts to generate leads for realtors:

1. **Use a Social Media Management Tool:** Social media management tools, such as Hootsuite, Buffer, or Sprout Social, allow realtors to schedule and publish content across multiple social media platforms, including Facebook, Instagram, LinkedIn, and Twitter. These tools also allow realtors to track analytics, such as engagement and reach, to measure the effectiveness of their content.

2. **Automate Repetitive Tasks:** Many social media management tools have automation features. Automation features allow realtors to automate repetitive tasks, such as sending direct messages to new followers. This can save time and effort and allow realtors to focus on more important tasks, such as creating valuable content and engaging with potential clients.

3. **Use a CRM Tool:** Customer Relationship Management (CRM) tools like Salesforce or HubSpot allow realtors to track and manage their leads and clients. These tools can integrate with social media management tools, allowing realtors to see social media activity and interactions with leads and clients.

4. **Use a Lead Generation Tool:** Lead generation tools like Leadformly or Leadpages allow realtors to create landing pages and forms. These are used to capture leads from social media. These tools can also be integrated with CRM tools, allowing realtors to track and manage leads automatically.

5. **Schedule Posts In Advance:** Many social media management tools allow realtors to schedule posts in advance. This can be a great way to save time and ensure that your social media accounts are consistently active.

6. **Use Analytics To Track Performance:** Social media management tools provide analytics that can help realtors track the performance of their social media accounts. Helping realtors understand which content types resonate with their audience and which strategies work best to generate leads.

Do some research, and find what tools are going to work best for you and your business.

## 9. SHARE VIRAL CONTENT

Content is crucial for realtors to share on social media to generate leads and grow their business.

Here are a few examples of the best types of content for realtors to share on social media:

1. **Tips For Buyers And Sellers:** Share tips and advice for buyers and sellers to help them navigate the real estate process. This can include information on preparing for a home inspection, staging a home for sale, and negotiating a purchase or sale.

2. **Real Estate Terms:** It's great to share definitions and explanations of common real estate terms. This can help educate potential clients and establish you as a knowledgeable and trustworthy authority in the industry.

3. **FAQ:** Share frequently asked questions about the real estate process, including information on the home buying and selling process, mortgage rates, and the role of a realtor.

4. **Infographics:** Share infographics that provide helpful information and tips on buying or selling a home. Infographics are a great way to convey complex information in an easy-to-understand format.

5. **Quotes:** Share quotes related to the real estate industry or inspiring people to take action when buying or selling a home. Quotes can be a great way to connect with potential clients and build trust.

6. **Testimonials:** Share testimonials from satisfied clients. Testimonials can be a great way to build credibility and trust with potential clients.

7. **Virtual Tours:** Share virtual tours of your listings. Tours can be a great way to showcase properties and give potential clients a sense of what it would be like to live there.

8. **Industry News:** Share news and updates about the real estate industry. This can include new laws, market trends, and other information that can be helpful for potential clients.

9. **Home Improvement Tips:** Share tips and advice on improving your home, including information on landscaping, interior design, and home repairs.

10. **Personal Stories:** Share personal stories about your experiences as a realtor. This can be a great way to connect with potential clients and build trust.

Realtors can share many types of content on social media to generate leads and grow their businesses.

- Sharing tips for buyers and sellers
- Explain real estate terms
- Answer FAQs
- Showcase infographics
- Quotes
- Testimonials,
- Virtual tours
- Display industry news
- Share home improvement tips
- Use personal stories.

Realtors can educate potential clients and establish themselves as trustworthy and knowledgeable authority in the industry. It's important to be consistent and share valuable content that resonates with your target audience.

If you need our done-for-you social media posts, you can also go to https://soldouthouses.com/365doneforyoucontent to grab your copy for a discount.

## ADDITIONAL IDEAS

Here are some ways you can generate leads for your real estate business through social media.

1. **Use Instagram and Facebook to showcase your listings.** Share high-quality photos and videos of your listings, and use relevant hashtags to make them more discoverable. You can also share behind-the-scenes footage of open houses or walkthroughs to give potential buyers a better sense of the property.

2. **Utilize Instagram and Facebook stories to share testimonials from satisfied clients**. This is a great way to build trust and credibility with potential buyers.

3. **Leverage Twitter to share industry news and tips.** You can use Twitter to share news about the real estate market and offer advice and tips for buyers and sellers. Doing this will help position you as a thought leader in the industry.

4. **Utilize LinkedIn to connect with other real estate professionals.** LinkedIn is a great platform for networking and building relationships with real estate agents, mortgage brokers, and industry professionals.

5. **Run social media ads to target specific demographics**. Instagram, Facebook, and Twitter all offer targeted advertising options. You can use these to reach specific audiences based on demographics such as age, location, and interests.

6. **Use Instagram and Facebook live videos to give virtual tours of your listings.** In times of pandemic or social distancing can be a great way to give potential buyers a sense of the property without them having to leave their homes.

7. **Use social media to host virtual open houses.** You can use Facebook Live or Instagram Live to host a virtual open house, which can be a great way to generate interest in a property.

Using these strategies, you can effectively generate your real estate business leads through social media. Remember, being consistent in your social media efforts and engaging with your followers is important. This will help build relationships and trust, which is essential in the real estate industry.

# MARKETING WITH YOUR WEBSITE

## WHY DO YOU NEED A WEBSITE?

In today's digital age, having a website is crucial for any business, including real estate. If you're a realtor and still need to get a website, it's time to build one.

A website lets you showcase your listings, services, and credentials to potential clients. It can help you reach a wider audience and attract more leads. A website also helps establish credibility and trust with your clients, demonstrating that you are a professional and reputable agent.

Once you have your website up and running you will soon see it as a powerful marketing tool. You can use it to generate leads through contact forms, property search functionality, and email sign-ups. You can also use it to share industry news, insights, and testimonials from satisfied clients.

A website is a great way to stay in touch with your clients. You can send regular updates and newsletters to keep your clients informed about new listings, market trends, and other relevant information.

Another benefit of having a website is that it can help you stand out in a crowded market. Many realtors rely on traditional marketing methods such as newspaper ads, flyers, and brochures. Still, a website allows you to showcase your unique selling points and differentiate yourself from the competition.

Lastly, a website can be a great tool to build your brand and make you your area's go-to agent. By using your website, you can create a strong online presence, making it easier for people to find you, remember you, and recommend you to others.

Owning a website is essential for any realtor. It can help you reach a wider audience, attract more leads, establish credibility, and differentiate yourself from the competition.

To take advantage of our done-for-you website and sales funnels, visit https://soldouthouses.com/easyfunnel to learn more.

## 10. ADD A TOUCH OF PROFESSIONALISM TO YOUR WEBSITE

After building a website for your real estate business, it's important to take the next step and ensure that it looks and functions professionally. A professionally designed website can make a big difference in how potential clients perceive your business and ultimately lead to more leads and sales.

One of the most important aspects of a professional website is its design. A well-designed website should be visually appealing, easy to navigate, and provide a great user experience. It should also be responsive and work seamlessly across different devices, such as desktop computers, tablets, and smartphones. A professional web designer can help you create an aesthetically pleasing website optimized for conversions.

Another important aspect of a professional website is its content. Your website should include detailed information about your listings, services, and credentials. It should also be easy to read and understand. A professional copywriter can help you create compelling and informative content that engages your visitors and encourages them to take action.

Additionally, a professional website should be secure and fast. It should be protected by a valid SSL certificate and optimized for speed. Ensuring your visitors' personal information is protected, and your website loads quickly can improve the user experience and help increase conversions.

A professional web developer can help you maintain and update your website regularly.

Lastly, a professional website should be regularly updated.

This includes:

- Updating your listings.
- Adding new blog posts.
- Ensuring that your website is compatible with the latest technologies.

A professionally designed website can significantly impact how potential clients perceive your business. It should be visually appealing, easy to navigate, responsive, secure, and fast. Additionally, it should have great content, be regularly updated, and be optimized for conversions. Investing in a professional web designer and developer will help you create a website that will help you stand out from the competition and generate more leads and sales.

## 11. GO FOR MOBILE OPTIMIZATION

In today's digital age, having a mobile-optimized website is crucial for any real estate business. With more and more people accessing the internet on their smartphones and tablets, realtors need to ensure that their website is optimized for mobile devices.

A mobile-optimized website for real estate businesses is designed to work seamlessly on smaller screens. Making it easy for visitors to navigate and find the information they need about properties, services, and contact information. This includes larger text, buttons, and a layout that adjusts to fit the screen size. With a mobile-optimized website, visitors can view your listings, read your content, and contact you easily, regardless of their device.

Mobile optimization also helps improve the user experience for real estate businesses. A mobile-optimized website will load faster and be more responsive, which can help keep visitors engaged and reduce bounce rates. Additionally, mobile optimization will help improve your search engine rankings, as Google and other search engines favor mobile-friendly websites.

Another benefit of mobile optimization for real estate businesses is that it can help you reach a wider audience. Many potential clients access the internet on their mobile devices, and a mobile-optimized website ensures you are not missing out on these potential leads.

A mobile-optimized website will help you stay ahead of the competition in the real estate business. As more and more people access the internet on their mobile devices, it's becoming increasingly important for realtors to have mobile-optimized websites. A mobile-optimized website should ensure your business is not left behind in the mobile era.

Mobile optimization is crucial for any realtor looking to establish a strong online presence and reach a wider audience in the real estate business. It will improve user experience and search engine rankings and ensure your business is not left behind in the mobile era. If your website is not yet mobile-optimized, it's time to take the necessary steps to ensure it is.

## 12. Optimize Your Website for Local Searches (Local SEO)

Optimizing your website for local searches is an important step for realtors looking to attract more leads and increase their online visibility. When potential clients search for real estate agents or properties in their area, your website needs to appear at the top of the search results.

One of the first steps in optimizing your website for local searches is to ensure that your website has accurate and complete contact information. This includes your name, address, phone number, and email address. You should display this information on your website and ensure it is displayed consistently across all your online listings and directories.

Another important aspect of local SEO is to include relevant keywords in your website's content, titles, and meta descriptions. For example, suppose you are a realtor in Los Angeles. In that case, you should include keywords such as "Los Angeles real estate," "homes for sale in Los Angeles," and "LA real estate agent" throughout your website. This will help search engines understand the focus and location of your business.

Another critical step is to claim and verify your Google My Business listing. Google My Business is a free listing service that allows businesses to manage their online presence across Google, including Search and Maps. By claiming and verifying your listing, you can ensure that your business information is accurate and up-to-date, making it easier for potential clients to find you.

You can boost your website's SEO by creating and optimizing local listings on directories such as Yelp, Yellow Pages, and Angie's List. This will help your business show up in local search results and directories, making it easier for potential clients to find you.

Tips to help your website show at the top:

- Include accurate contact information
- Use relevant keywords
- Claim and verify your google MY Business listing
- Optimize your local listing.

Optimizing your website for local searches is essential for realtors looking to attract more leads and increase their online visibility.

## 13. DEVELOP AN ATTRACTIVE WEBSITE WITH GREAT UI AND UX.

An attractive and user-friendly website can be a powerful tool for realtors looking to generate leads and grow their business. A website with great UI and UX (user interface and user experience) can help realtors establish themselves as a trusted and credible resource for potential clients.

One way to develop an attractive website is by investing in a professional website design. This process can include hiring a web designer to create a visually appealing and professional-looking website.

It's important to ensure that the website is mobile-friendly, as more and more people are accessing the internet on their smartphones and tablets.

Another way to develop an attractive website is by focusing on user experience. This can include ensuring that the website is easy to navigate, with clear and concise information about your services.

It's also important to test the website's speed and responsiveness, so clients don't have to wait for pages to load. There is nothing worse than waiting for a page to load.

In addition, realtors can also invest in a property search functionality on their website, which allows users to search for properties based on location, price, and other criteria. This is a powerful tool for generating leads, as users can easily find properties matching their search criteria.

Don't forget to regularly update and maintain your website:

Keep up-to-date:

- Adding new content
- Blog posts
- Articles
- Videos
- Fixing any technical issues

By regularly updating and maintaining your website, realtors can ensure that it remains relevant and useful to potential clients. An attractive and user-friendly website with great UI and UX can be a powerful tool for realtors looking to generate leads and grow their business.

## 14. ADD CUSTOMER TESTIMONIALS TO YOUR WEBSITE

Reviews and testimonials are powerful tools for real estate agents looking to generate more social proof and establish their businesses as reliable. They provide a way for potential buyers and sellers to hear from others who have had a positive experience with your business.

This can help build trust and credibility, making it more likely for them to consider using your services.

One way to use reviews and testimonials on your real estate website is by highlighting them prominently on your homepage or a dedicated page. Making them more visible to potential buyers and sellers can make it easy for them to read through multiple reviews simultaneously.

Another way to use reviews and testimonials is by including them in your marketing materials, such as brochures, flyers, and email campaigns. This can help reinforce your business's positive reputation and provide potential buyers and sellers with additional social proof.

It's also important to ask your clients for reviews and testimonials after a transaction is completed. You can also use platforms such as Google Reviews, Yelp, and Zillow, to gather more reviews and testimonials, as the public widely recognizes them.

It would help if you asked for specific feedback on your services when gathering reviews and testimonials. This feedback can help to provide potential buyers and sellers with a more detailed understanding of the level of service they can expect to receive from you.

Furthermore you can include pictures or videos of your clients giving testimonials. This will make them more relatable and believable and help potential buyers and sellers put a face and a name to the testimonial.

## 15. POST A VIRTUAL PROPERTY TOUR ON YOUR WEBSITE

Virtual property tours can be a valuable tool for realtors looking to stand out in a competitive market. Virtual tours can help potential buyers envision themselves living in the space by providing a detailed, interactive look at a property, leading to increased interest and, ultimately, a sale.

One way to create a virtual tour is by using a 360-degree camera to capture footage of the property. These cameras can create an immersive experience that allows viewers to explore the property at their own pace. The footage from these cameras can be edited together to create a seamless tour that highlights the property's best features. Another way to create a virtual tour is to use a 3D camera to scan and create a 3D model of the property. This allows for even more detailed and realistic visualizations of the property.

In addition to adding virtual tours to your website, you can also share the tours on social media platforms to reach a wider audience. By sharing the tours on platforms like Facebook and Instagram, you can attract potential buyers who may not have found your listing otherwise.

Virtual tours are a great way to showcase a property's features and can be especially helpful for buyers who cannot physically visit the property. They are also great for out-of-state or international buyers, as they can get a feel for the property without traveling. Virtual tours can also save realtors time and money, as they don't need to schedule and conduct physical property tours constantly.

Want to stand out? Virtual property tours on your website can set you apart from other realtors. Virtual tours give potential buyers a detailed, interactive look at your listing properties. It can save time and money and can also attract a wider audience. This is a proven way to make your listings more attractive and increase the chances of closing a sale.

## 16. BOOST YOUR WEBSITE TRAFFIC WITH SEO BACKLINKING

SEO backlinking is a powerful technique that can help realtors generate leads and boost their online visibility. What are backlinks? Backlinks are links from other websites that point to your website. When other websites link to your website, it signals to search engines that it is valuable and credible. This can help your website rank higher in search engine results pages (SERPs). Making it more likely that potential clients will find your website when searching for real estate-related keywords.

One way to generate backlinks is by creating valuable and informative content on your website. This can include blog posts, articles, infographics, and videos that provide helpful information to potential clients. When other websites find your content valuable, they may link to it, which can help boost your website's visibility.

Another way to generate backlinks is by contacting other websites and asking them to link to your website. This includes reaching out to other realtors, mortgage brokers, home inspectors, and other professionals in the real estate industry.

Reach out to local businesses and organizations, such as furniture stores, home staging companies, and interior design firms. These companies are great resources.

To generate backlinks, you can also participate in online communities, such as forums and discussion boards. By providing valuable information and engaging in conversations, you can establish yourself as a trusted and credible resource, which can lead to other websites linking to your website.

Create and share infographics, videos, webinars, e-books, and other types of content that can be shared on other websites and social media platforms. Together this can help generate backlinks while also providing value to potential clients.

SEO backlinking can be a powerful technique for realtors looking to generate leads and boost their online visibility.

- Create valuable and informative content.
- Reach out to other websites.
- Participate in online communities sharing different types of content.

Realtors who generate backlinks to help their website rank higher attract more potential leads to their real estate business.

## 17. CAPTURING LEADS WITH YOUR WEBSITE.

Capturing leads with a website is essential to a realtor's lead generation strategy. Here are a few strategies for capturing leads with a website:

1. **Use Lead Capture Forms:** Incorporate lead capture forms on your website, such as contact forms, request consultation forms, or sign-up for newsletter forms. These forms should be placed in prominent locations like the homepage or property listings page. They should be easy to fill out and submit.

2. **Offer Valuable Resources:** Provide valuable resources on your website, such as e-books, guides, or webinars. These resources should be relevant to your target audience. They should require visitors to provide their contact information to access them.

3. **Optimize For SEO:** Optimize your website for search engine optimization (SEO) to make it more likely to be found by potential clients. This includes using keywords, meta tags, and other SEO best practices.

4. **Use Chatbots:** Implement chatbots on your website to interact with visitors, answer their questions and collect their information. Chatbots can help you engage with potential leads and gather their contact information in real time.

5. **Use Landing Pages:** Create dedicated landing pages for specific campaigns or services. These pages should be optimized for conversions, with clear calls to action and minimal distractions.

6. **Use Retargeting:** Use retargeting to show ads to visitors who have already interacted with your website. This will help you stay top of mind with leads and increase the chances of conversion.

7. **Use Lead Magnets:** Offer lead magnets such as free consultations, property valuations, or market reports in exchange for contact information. Making this a great way to capture leads and establish yourself as a valuable resource.

8. **Use Analytics:** Use analytics to track your website's performance and identify improvement areas. Helping you understand which pages drive the most conversions and which areas of your website need more attention.

9. **Use A/B Testing:** Use A/B testing to test different website versions and determine which elements are most effective in converting leads. This can include different testing headlines, images, and calls to action.

As you can see, having and utilizing your website is key to success.

# BUILD YOUR
# SALES FUNNEL

## WHY YOU NEED A SALES FUNNEL

As a realtor, using sales funnels can be a powerful tool for capturing and nurturing leads. A sales funnel is a marketing strategy that guides potential buyers through the process of purchasing a property, from initial awareness to closing the sale.

To start, you can create a strong online presence by having a professional website and active social media accounts. This will make it easy for potential buyers to find and contact you. You can also offer valuable resources such as home-buying guides or market reports to attract potential buyers and establish yourself as a valuable resource.

Once you have attracted potential buyers, you can use lead capture forms on your website and email campaigns to collect their contact information. This will allow you to add them to your email list and begin nurturing your leads.

Next, you can use targeted emails and personalized follow-ups to engage potential buyers. Provide them with valuable information and resources, such as upcoming open houses or market updates, to continue establishing yourself as a valuable resource. This will also help to build trust and credibility with your potential buyers.

As potential buyers move further down the sales funnel, you can use techniques such as initial phone calls or meetings to qualify your leads. This will allow you to identify which potential buyers are ready to move forward in the sales process and focus your efforts on those individuals.

Finally, you can use open houses, virtual tours, and face-to-face meetings to help potential buyers decide and close the sale. In addition, continue building a relationship with your clients, as it can generate future business from repeat clients or referrals.

Using a sales funnel, you can effectively capture and nurture leads and increase your chances of closing a sale.

If you want to take advantage of our done-for-you sales funnel system, go to https://soldouthouses.com/easyfunnel/ to learn more.

## 18. CREATE A LEAD MAGNET

A lead magnet is a valuable piece of content or offers used to attract potential clients and generate leads in the real estate industry. Real estate agents can use a variety of lead magnets to attract potential clients and build their pipeline of leads.

One effective lead magnet for realtors is a free home valuation. Creating a landing page on their website where clients can enter their property information and request a free home valuation. Once the client submits their information, the realtor can follow up with them to discuss their property and potential listing, which can lead to a successful sale. Realtors can also promote free valuation through social media, email marketing, and targeted online advertising.

Another lead magnet that realtors can use is a free home buying or selling guide. These guides can provide valuable information to potential clients about the home buying or selling process, including the steps involved, what to expect, and tips for getting the best price for a property. Realtors can promote these guides through their website, social media, and email marketing and offer them during consultations with potential clients.

Realtors can also offer a free consultation as a lead magnet. During the consultation, realtors can discuss the client's needs and tailor their services accordingly. You can help establish the realtor as an expert in the field and build trust with potential clients. Realtors can promote the free consultation through their website, social media, and email marketing.

Another popular lead magnet is an e-book or whitepaper that provides valuable information on a specific topic, such as how to stage a home for sale or find the perfect one. These e-books can be promoted through the realtor's website, social media, and email marketing. They can be used to establish the realtor as an expert in the field.

Realtors can also use virtual tours or virtual open houses as lead magnets. These can be promoted through their website, social media, and email marketing and can be used to attract potential clients interested in viewing a property but unable to do so in person.

In addition to the above lead magnets, realtors can also use online quizzes, webinars, and free reports as lead magnets. These can attract potential clients and generate leads by providing valuable Information on a specific topic.

It's worth noting that for all the lead magnets, realtors should collect the client's contact information, such as their name and email address, to follow up with them and nurture the lead. Realtors can also use lead magnets as a way to segment their leads by providing different lead magnets for different stages of the buying or selling process.

Additionally, realtors should make sure to collect the client's contact information and use lead magnets as a way to segment their leads.

## 19. FREE BUYER & SELLER GUIDES

Another way for realtors to generate leads is by offering free buyer and seller guides. These guides can provide valuable information to potential clients interested in buying or selling a property and help establish the realtor as an expert in the field.

Realtors can use the guides as a lead magnet by requiring clients to enter their contact information to access the guide. This way, realtors can build a list of potential clients who are interested in buying or selling a property.

To create a buyer guide, realtors can include information on the home buying process, including the steps involved, what to expect, and tips for finding the perfect home. The guide can also include information on financing options, such as mortgages and home equity loans. Additionally, realtors can include information on the local real estate market, including current trends and statistics.

To create a seller guide, realtors can include information on the home selling process, including the steps involved, what to expect, and tips for getting the best price for a property. The guide can also include information on preparing a home for sale, such as staging and repairs. Additionally, realtors can include information on the local real estate market, including current trends and statistics.

Once the buyer and seller guides are created, realtors can promote them through various marketing channels. They can include a link to the guides on their website and promote them through social media, email marketing, and targeted online advertising. Realtors can also offer guides in person during consultations with potential clients.

Realtors can establish themselves as experts in the field and build trust with potential clients by providing valuable information about the buying and selling process. Additionally, the guides can provide potential clients with a clear understanding of what to expect when buying or selling a home, leading to more successful transactions.

Furthermore, realtors can generate leads by offering to send the guide via email regularly. This way, they can keep in touch with potential clients and remind them of the realtor's expertise and services. Realtors can also include a call to action in the guide, such as a link to schedule a consultation or request more information.

## 20. FREE EVALUATION

Generating leads is a crucial aspect of the real estate business. One effective way for realtors to do so is by offering a free property evaluation service. This service can help attract potential clients interested in selling their property but unsure of its value. Realtors can demonstrate their expertise and establish trust with potential clients by providing a free evaluation, which can lead to successful sales.

One way to offer a free property evaluation is by creating a landing page on a realtor's website, where clients can enter their property information and request an evaluation. This landing page should be easy to find and navigate and clearly state the benefits of requesting an evaluation. For example, realtors can highlight that the evaluation will give clients an accurate estimate of their property's value. Don't forget to include valuable insights on increasing its value before listing it for sale.

In addition to having a landing page on their website, realtors can promote the free evaluation service through various marketing channels. Social media platforms like Facebook, Instagram, and Twitter can reach a large audience. At the same time, email marketing can target specific groups of potential clients. Realtors can also use targeted online advertising to reach potential clients in their area who may be interested in selling their property.

Once a potential client has requested a free evaluation, realtors should follow up with them as soon as possible. This follow-up should include a personalized message that thanks the client for requesting an evaluation and provides them with a clear timeline of when they can expect to receive the evaluation. Realtors should also provide clients with their contact information so that they can reach out with any questions or concerns.

The evaluation itself should be thorough and professional. Realtors should take the time to visit the property and take detailed notes on its condition, size, and location. They should also research comparable sales in the area and use that information to determine the property's value. Once the evaluation is complete, realtors should provide the client with a detailed report that includes the property's estimated value and recommendations on increasing its value before listing it for sale.

Realtors can demonstrate their expertise and establish trust with potential clients by offering a free property evaluation service, leading to successful sales and generating more realtor business leads. Additionally, providing a free evaluation can be a good start for building a relationship and trust with clients that can benefit the future business.

## 21. FREE CONSULTATIONS

A consultation is a meeting or call during which a realtor can discuss a potential client's needs and provide valuable information about the real estate process. By offering a free consultation, realtors can establish themselves as experts in the field and build trust with potential clients, which can lead to successful sales.

There are several ways for realtors to offer free consultations. One way is to create a landing page on their website where potential clients can schedule a consultation. This landing page should be easy to find and navigate and should clearly state the benefits of scheduling a consultation. For example, a realtor can highlight that the consultation will provide the client with valuable information about the real estate process and help them make informed decisions.

In addition to having a landing page on their website, realtors can promote free consultations through various marketing channels. Social media platforms like Facebook, Instagram, and Twitter can be used to reach a large audience. In contrast, email marketing can target specific groups of potential clients. Realtors can also use targeted online advertising to reach potential clients in their area who may be interested in buying or selling a property.

Once a potential client has scheduled a consultation, the realtor should prepare for the meeting by researching the client's needs and the local real estate market. During the consultation, the realtor should listen actively to the client's needs, ask questions, and provide valuable information about the real estate process. They should also discuss the potential listing, what the client can expect from the realtor and the process.

Additionally, realtors should provide the client with their contact information and follow up with them after the consultation to discuss the next steps. This follow-up can include a personalized message that thanks the client for scheduling the consultation and provides a clear timeline of when they can expect to hear back from the realtor.

Realtors can demonstrate their expertise and build trust with potential clients by offering free consultations. This can ultimately lead to successful sales and help generate more leads for the realtor's business. Additionally, providing a free consultation makes a good start for building a relationship and trust with the client that can benefit future business.

## 22. FREE WEBINARS

Webinars are a powerful tool for realtors to generate leads and promote their services. Realtors can educate potential clients on the current real estate market by hosting a webinar. You can offer valuable tips for buying or selling a property and provide information about their services. Promoting it effectively and ensuring that the content is relevant and valuable to the audience is key to a successful webinar.

To promote the webinar, realtors can start by creating a landing page on their website that provides all the details about the event, including the date and time, and a sign-up form for attendees to register. They can also create a Facebook event and invite their past clients and potential leads to attend.

Realtors can reach out to their past clients and potential leads through email, text messages, and social media to inform them about the upcoming webinar. These messages highlight the webinar's value, such as the opportunity to learn about the current real estate market or tips on selling a property quickly.

During the webinar, the realtor should focus on providing valuable information that will interest the attendees. For example, they can discuss the current state of the real estate market, including trends, statistics, and forecasts. They can also share tips and strategies for buying or selling a property, such as finding the right real estate agent, preparing a property for sale, and negotiating a successful deal.

At the end of the webinar, the realtor can offer a call-to-action for attendees to contact them for more information or to schedule a consultation. Making this a great opportunity for the realtor to convert leads into clients. They can also offer a special promotion or incentive for those who sign up for a consultation within a certain time frame.

Finally, the realtor can record the webinar and use the recording as a lead-generation tool on their website and social media channels. You can use this recording to promote the realtor's services to those unable to attend the live event or to anyone interested in learning more about the current real estate market.

Webinars are a powerful tool for realtors to generate leads and promote their services. By effectively promoting the event, providing valuable content, and offering a call-to-action, realtors can convert leads into clients. And by recording the webinar, they can continue to generate leads even after the event is over.

## 23. OFFERING FREE BOOKS/ EBOOKS

Realtors can generate leads with free books or ebooks by creating a valuable resource that provides valuable information about the real estate market or the home buying or selling process. The book or ebook can be offered as a free download on the realtor's website, social media channels, or online marketplaces.

To promote the book or ebook, realtors can start by creating a landing page on their website. Provide all the details about the resource, including a description and a sign-up form for the download. They can also create a social media campaign that promotes the book or ebook and encourages people to sign up.

Realtors can also reach out to their past clients and potential leads through email, text messages, and social media to let them know about the free book or ebook. In these messages, they should highlight the value of the resource, such as tips and strategies for buying or selling a property or the current state of the real estate market.

Once the book or ebook is downloaded, the realtor can use it to generate leads by including calls to action throughout the book or ebook. Offer a free consultation or provide a contact form for readers to get in touch.

Realtors can also use the book or ebook to establish themselves as an expert in their field, which can help build trust and credibility with potential clients. Use this ebook as a lead-generation tool on social media and other online platforms. Realtors can promote the resource and encourage people to download it.

By offering a free book or ebook can be a powerful way for realtors to generate leads. Realtors can convert readers into leads by providing valuable information and including calls to action. They can reach a wider audience and generate more leads by promoting the resource on their website and social media channels.

# CONTENT
# MARKETING IDEAS

## WHY CONTENT MARKETING

Content marketing is a powerful tool for generating leads in the real estate industry. Creating and sharing valuable informative content can attract potential buyers and sellers to your business. Establish yourself as a proven leader in the industry.

Here are some ways you can use content marketing to generate leads for your real estate business:

1. **Create A Blog:** Creating a blog on your website is a great way to share valuable information with potential buyers and sellers. You can use your blog to share information about the local real estate market, tips for buying or selling a home, and information about financing options.

2. **Use Social Media:** Social media platforms such as Facebook, Instagram, and Twitter are powerful tools for sharing content and generating leads. You can use these platforms to share your blog posts, listings, and other valuable content to attract potential buyers and sellers.

3. **Create Infographics:** Infographics are a great way to share valuable information visually. You can use infographics to share information about the local real estate market, tips for buying or selling a home, and financing options.

4. **Use Videos:** Videos are a powerful tool for generating leads. You can use videos to showcase your listings, provide virtual tours, and share valuable information about the local real estate market.

5. **Use E-Books and Whitepapers:** E-books and whitepapers are great for sharing information in a more comprehensive format. You can use e-books and whitepapers to share information about the local real estate market, tips for buying or selling a home, and financing options.

6. **Create A Newsletter:** Create a newsletter that you can send out to potential buyers and sellers. This will allow you to share your latest listings, valuable information about the local real estate market, and tips for buying or selling a home.
7. **Use SEO**: Optimize your content for search engines by using keywords in your title tags, meta tags, and content. This will help your content rank higher in search engine results and attract organic traffic to your website.

If you want to take advantage of our done-for-you social media posts, you can visit https://soldouthouses.com/365doneforyoucontent to learn more.

## 24. TAKE ADVANTAGE OF VIDEO MARKETING

Realtors can generate leads with video marketing by creating short videos that showcase their listings. Be sure to provide valuable information about the real estate market or offer tips and advice for buying or selling a property. These videos can be promoted on the realtor's website, social media channels, and video-sharing platforms such as YouTube, Vimeo, and TikTok.

Not only does video allow you to showcase properties in a more engaging and dynamic way, but it also allows potential buyers and sellers to get a sense of your personality and approach to real estate.

One effective strategy for realtors is to create video tours of properties you have listed. These tours can be used on your website, social media, and other marketing channels to give potential buyers a sense of the property's layout and features. You can also create videos that offer tips and advice for buying or selling a home, such as how to stage a home for a showing or navigate the home-buying process.

Another effective strategy is to create videos that highlight your local community and the lifestyle it offers. These videos can showcase local amenities, events, and attractions and help potential buyers envision themselves living in the area. You can also use videos to introduce yourself and your team and share client testimonials.

A live video is also a great tool for realtors. Live video lets you interact with your audience in real time, answer questions, and provide a more personal touch. For example, you can use live video to give virtual tours of open houses and to host Q&A sessions. Let potential buyers ask you about the buying or selling process.

Another interesting idea for realtors is to create videos that show a day in the life of a real estate agent. This type of video is a great way to give potential clients an inside look at your work and can help establish you as an authority and a professional in your field.

You can use video marketing to boost your search engine optimization efforts. Add keywords and meta tags to your videos and publish them on video hosting sites such as YouTube.

## 25. BLOGGING

Blogs can be a valuable addition to your real estate agent advertising efforts. While they may provide little results, the long-term benefits of having a blog can be well worth the effort. Blogs can be used to provide valuable information to potential buyers and sellers, showcase your expertise and build a relationship with your audience. This can establish you as a trusted source of information and make it more likely that they will turn to you when they are ready to buy or sell a property.

When creating a blog, it's important to focus on providing relevant information to your audience. For example, you can write about local market conditions, tips for buying or selling a property, or even lifestyle and design ideas for home improvement. By providing this content, you can demonstrate your knowledge and expertise, making it more likely that potential buyers and sellers will turn to you for advice.

Another way to use a blog to support your real estate agent advertising efforts is by featuring listings on your blog. You can write about each property's unique features and benefits and include high-quality photos. This can generate interest in the property and make it more likely that potential buyers will schedule a viewing.

Blogs can also be a great way to reach a wider audience. By sharing your blog posts on social media and other online platforms, you can attract more visitors to your website and increase your visibility. Additionally, by including links to your website and contact information in your blog posts, you can make it easy for potential buyers and sellers to get in touch with you.

Blogging is also a great way to build a relationship with your audience. By regularly posting content, you can establish yourself as a thought leader in your field and show that you are an expert in the local market. This will help to establish trust and loyalty with your audience, making it more likely that they will turn to you when they are ready to buy or sell a property.

You can also use your blog to showcase your community involvement and highlight the local events and businesses in the area. Realtors can help potential buyers see the appeal of the neighborhood and community and make them more likely to consider purchasing a property in the area.

## 26. RUNNING A PODCAST

Running a podcast can be a highly effective strategy for real estate professionals looking to connect with their audience and promote their business in a non-traditional way. Podcasts are a powerful tool for marketing because they have a large and dedicated audience, with more than 380 million listeners worldwide.

Realtors can use podcasts by creating a show that focuses on the local real estate market. Including interviews with local experts, market analysis, and tips and advice for buyers and sellers. By positioning yourself as a knowledgeable and trustworthy source of information on the local real estate market, you can establish yourself as an authority in the eyes of potential clients.

Another approach is to create a podcast that focuses on personal development and the mindset of successful real estate professionals. This can include interviews with successful agents and industry leaders, as well as tips and strategies for building a successful career in real estate. You can attract a dedicated and engaged audience of real estate professionals and other business owners by providing valuable insights and inspiration.

Podcasts can also be a great way to connect with potential clients and build relationships. You can use your podcast to showcase your listed properties, provide virtual tours, introduce yourself and your team, and share client testimonials.

Live podcasting is also a great tool for realtors. Live podcasting allows you to interact with your audience in real time, answer questions, and provide a more personal touch. Use live podcasting to give virtual tours of open houses and to host Q&A sessions where potential buyers can ask you about the buying or selling process.

Another idea for realtors is to create a podcast focusing on a specific niche or target market. For example, you can create a podcast for first-time home buyers or luxury property buyers. By focusing on a specific niche, you can attract a highly targeted and engaged audience that is more likely to become a client.

## 27. OFFER VIRTUAL TOURS TO YOUR CLIENTS

Virtual tours are a powerful tool for realtors looking to showcase their listings uniquely and engagingly. Unlike traditional photos, virtual tours provide a 360-degree view of a property, allowing buyers to fully immerse themselves in the space and imagine themselves living there. This can be especially beneficial for properties that are difficult to visualize, such as those with an unusual layout or a large lot.

There are several different ways to create a virtual tour. One popular option is to use a 360-degree camera to capture the property, then upload the images to a virtual tour platform. Another option is to use a combination of photos and videos to create a virtual walkthrough of the property. Some platforms also offer the ability to create a virtual tour using only photos, stitching them together to create a panoramic view.

One of the biggest advantages of virtual tours is that they allow buyers to explore a property from the comfort of their own homes.

Saving much time for buyers and realtors, eliminating the need for multiple viewings. Virtual tours can also be shared easily on websites, social media, and other online platforms, making it easier for buyers to view properties remotely.

Another advantage of virtual tours is that they can help to generate more interest in a property. The immersive nature of virtual tours can make a property more memorable, leading to more viewings and, ultimately, more offers. Virtual tours can also be a great way to highlight the unique features of a property, such as a large backyard, a beautiful view, or a unique architectural design.

In addition to being an effective tool for showcasing listings, virtual tours can also be beneficial for realtors looking to build their brand. By providing virtual tours of properties that you have listed, you can demonstrate your expertise and attention to detail. This can attract more buyers and sellers to your business.

Another strategy for virtual tours is to provide floor plans along with the tour. This can give buyers a sense of how the property is laid out and how the different spaces are connected. It also allows buyers to imagine how the space could be used and what furniture could be placed where.

## 28. REPURPOSING EXISTING CONTENT

Repurposing existing content is a cost-effective and efficient way to increase the reach and engagement of your brand. By repurposing content in different formats, you can reach new audiences and appeal to a wider range of preferences. For example, you can break up a blog post into smaller, more focused posts that can be shared on social media. Or you can create a series of posts or videos covering different aspects of buying or selling. This can help increase engagement with existing audiences and attract new ones.

Another benefit of repurposing existing content is that it can help improve your search engine optimization (SEO). Creating multiple pieces of content targeting different keywords and phrases can increase visibility and drive more traffic to your website.

This can help establish your online presence and attract potential clients. You can build authority and expertise in the industry by consistently providing valuable, relevant, and informative content. Which is crucial for attracting new clients and building trust with existing ones.

There are several ways realtors can generate multiple pieces of content by repurposing existing content:

1. Break up a blog post into smaller, more focused posts that can be shared on social media.
2. Create a series of posts or videos that cover different aspects of the buying or selling process.
3. Turn a blog post into a video or podcast and vice versa.
4. Create infographics or other visual content to illustrate key points from a blog post
5. Create a slide presentation or webinar based on a blog post.
6. Use quotes or key takeaways from a blog post in social media posts.
7. Create a FAQ page or guide based on common questions or issues that come up in blog posts.
8. Use the content as a source for email marketing campaigns.

Repurposing existing content is an effective way for realtors to efficiently and effectively market their business and establish their authority and expertise in the industry. By repurposing content in different formats, you can reach new audiences and increase engagement with existing ones.

It can help improve your SEO, drive more traffic to your website and build trust with potential clients. So, instead of creating new content from scratch every time, take the time to repurpose your existing content and see how it can help you grow your business.

# OFFLINE
# MARKETING IDEAS

## WHY OFFLINE MARKETING?

While online marketing has become increasingly important in recent years, offline marketing should still be a part of a realtor's overall marketing strategy.

Here are a few reasons why:

1. **Reach a Wider Audience:** Despite what we think, not everyone is online. Offline marketing allows realtors to reach potential clients who may not be active on social media or searching for homes online.

2. **Target Specific Demographics:** Offline marketing allows realtors to target specific demographics, such as older adults or families, who may not be as active online.

3. **Create A Tangible Connection:** Offline marketing materials, such as business cards and brochures, provide a tangible connection for potential clients and help establish trust and credibility.

4. **Stand Out From The Competition:** With the rise of online marketing, offline marketing can help realtors stand out from the competition and make a memorable impression

5. **Cost-Effective:** Marketing this way can be cost-effective, especially compared to online marketing strategies such as paid advertising.

6. **Better ROI:** Offline marketing strategies such as door-to-door visits or direct mail can yield a better return on investment (ROI) than online marketing. Especially if it is targeted at the right audience.

7. **Branding:** It allows realtors to build their brand offline. Helping establish a sense of trust, credibility, and reliability with potential clients.

Overall, a well-rounded marketing strategy should include online and offline marketing efforts. While online marketing can effectively reach a wide audience and provide detailed information about properties, offline marketing can provide a personal touch. Those personal touches help establish trust and credibility with potential clients.

If you want access to our done-for-you online & offline marketing templates, visit https://soldouthouses.com/pro to check out our pro membership.

## 29. HOST OPEN HOUSES

Hosting open houses is a great marketing idea for realtors looking to generate leads and increase their visibility in the community. Open houses allow potential buyers to see a property in person and realtors to showcase their listings and services and build relationships with potential clients.

One of the main benefits of hosting open houses is that it allows potential buyers to see a property in person. They can walk through the property, ask questions, and get a sense of the layout and flow of the space. This can help them make a more informed decision about whether or not to make an offer.

The second most important reason for an open house is that you generate leads. By inviting potential buyers to an open house, you can collect their contact information and follow up with them in the future. This can help you build a database of potential clients who may be interested in buying a property in the future.

Hosting open houses can also be an effective way to build relationships with potential clients. By meeting with them in person, you can get to know them better, understand their needs and preferences, and provide them with personalized recommendations. This can help you establish yourself as a trusted advisor and make it more likely that they will come to you when they are ready to buy or sell a property.

Lastly, hosting open houses can also help you increase your visibility in the community. By inviting people to your open houses, you can introduce yourself to the community and show off your listings and services. This can help you build your brand and establish yourself as a reputable, experienced realtor.

Hosting open houses is a great marketing idea for realtors looking to generate leads, build relationships, and increase their visibility in the community. By allowing potential buyers to see a property in person, you can help them make a more informed decision about whether or not to make an offer and establish yourself as a trusted advisor.

## 30. OPTIMIZE YOUR OPEN HOUSES

Here are some tips for hosting a successful open house:

1. **Advertise The Open House:** Advertising your open house in local newspapers is a great outlet. Don't forget online classifieds and social media platforms. You can also use flyers and postcards to promote the open house.
2. **Make The Property Look Its Best**: Ensure the property is clean and well-maintained before the open house. Consider hiring a professional cleaner or stager to help make the property look its best. A fresh bouquet of flowers is always a nice touch.

3. **Provide Refreshments:** Provide refreshments such as coffee and snacks to make the open house more inviting for potential buyers. Be sure to avoid foods that leave crumbs!

4. **Make The Property Accessible:** Make sure the property is easy to access and well-lit. Ensure all doors and windows are unlocked and open to make it easier for potential buyers to navigate the property.

5. **Be Prepared To Answer Questions:** Be prepared to answer questions about the property, the neighborhood, and the local real estate market.

6. **Collect Contact Information:** Collect contact information from potential buyers so you can follow up with them after the open house. Try to make it fun, raffle a gift card, or chocolates.

7. **Use Virtual Open House:** In times of pandemic or social distancing, you can use virtual open houses. These give potential buyers a sense of the property without leaving their homes. You can use platforms like Zoom, Facebook Live, or Instagram Live to host the virtual open house and reach a wider audience.

8. **Follow Up With Potential Buyers:** Follow up with potential buyers after the open house to answer any further questions and schedule a showing if interested.

Following these tips, you can host a successful open house that generates your real estate business leads. Remember, an open house is a great opportunity to connect with potential buyers. It's vital to make a good impression and to be prepared to answer any questions they may have.

## 31. REAL ESTATE FRAMING

Framing is a powerful technique that can be used to generate leads in the real estate industry. It involves presenting information in a specific way that will make your prospects react in a desired manner, increasing the likelihood of conversions. Here are some ways you can use framing to generate leads for your real estate business:

1. **Use Scarcity To Create Urgency:** Scarcity is a powerful tool that can create urgency and drive conversions. For example, you can frame a listing as a "once-in-a-lifetime opportunity" or a "rare find" to create a sense of urgency among potential buyers.

2. **Use Social Proof To Build Trust:** Social proof is a powerful tool that can be used to build trust and credibility with potential buyers. For example, you can frame a listing as a "hot property" or a "popular choice among buyers" to create a sense of social proof and make it more appealing to potential buyers.

3. **Use Benefits To Highlight The Value Of A Property:** Highlighting the benefits of a property is an effective way to make it more appealing to potential buyers. For example, you can frame a property as a "great investment opportunity" or a "perfect family home" to highlight the benefits of the property and make it more appealing to potential buyers.

4. **Use Storytelling To Create Emotional Connection**: Storytelling is a powerful tool that can create an emotional connection with potential buyers. For example, you can frame a property as a "charming starter home" or a "luxurious retreat" to create an emotional connection with potential buyers and make the property more appealing.

5. **Use Comparisons To Highlight The Advantages Of A Property:** Comparisons are powerful tools highlighting a property's advantages. For example, you can frame a property as "more spacious than other homes in the neighborhood" or "more affordable than other properties" to make it stand out and appeal to potential buyers.

6. **Use Visual Aids To Make The Property Stand Out:** Visual aids such as high-quality images, videos, and virtual tours can be used to make a property stand out and appeal to potential buyers.

## 32. NETWORKING

Networking is a crucial aspect of any real estate business. It is a powerful tool that can help you generate leads, build relationships, and grow your business.

Here are some ways you can use networking to generate leads for your real estate business:

1. **Attend Networking Events:** Attend local networking events such as the chamber of commerce meetings, real estate industry conferences, and networking groups. These events provide an opportunity to meet other real estate professionals, build relationships, and generate leads.

2. **Join A Real Estate Association:** Joining a professional association such as the National Association of Realtors (NAR), or the local board of Realtors is a great way to network with other real estate professionals and generate leads.

3. **Leverage Social Media:** Social media platforms such as LinkedIn and Twitter are powerful networking tools. Connect with other real estate professionals, build relationships, and generate leads.

4. **Build Relationships With Other Professionals:** Building relationships with other professionals, such as mortgage brokers, home inspectors, and home stagers, can be a great way to generate leads. These professionals often work with buyers and sellers and can refer businesses to you.

5. **Leverage Your Sphere Of Influence:** Leverage your personal and professional network to generate leads. Your friends, family, and colleagues can be a great source of referrals.

6. **Use Referral Marketing:** Referral marketing is a powerful strategy that can be used to generate leads. Encourage satisfied clients to refer their friends and family to you and incentivize them to do so.

7. **Host Or Attend Open Houses Or Networking Events**: Hosting or attending open houses, or networking events can be a great way to meet potential clients and generate leads.

Using these networking strategies, you can effectively generate leads for your real estate business. Remember, networking is about building relationships. Focusing on building long-term relationships is important rather than just trying to close a sale.

Following these steps will help you generate more leads and grow your business over time.

## 33. ATTEND SEMINARS FOR FIRST-TIME BUYERS

Attending seminars for first-time buyers can be a great way to gain more in-depth information about the real estate market and connect with potential clients. There are several benefits to attending these types of seminars, both for the attendees and real estate professionals.

One of the biggest benefits of attending seminars for first-time buyers is that it allows people to get answers to all their questions related to real estate. Many first-time buyers have a lot of queries running through their minds, and seminars provide a great opportunity to get answers to these questions. In addition, being part of a group setting can generate more questions and ideas, which can benefit both the attendees and the real estate professionals leading the seminar.

As a real estate professional, you can also use these seminars to your advantage. One way to do this is by taking note of frequently asked questions by first-time buyers. This can help you identify common concerns and potential clients' confusion. By providing answers to these questions; you can generate more leads in the form of seminar attendees.

You can also use seminars as an opportunity to promote your services and connect with potential clients. By providing valuable information and answering questions, you can establish yourself as a knowledgeable and trustworthy expert in the field. This can help you attract new leads and build your business.

Another benefit of attending seminars for first-time buyers is that they can help you stay up-to-date with the latest trends and changes in the real estate market. Seminars often feature guest speakers and experts in the field. They can be an excellent way to learn about new developments, regulations, and best practices.

Attending seminars for first-time buyers is a smart move for real estate professionals looking to gain a deeper understanding of the market and connect with potential clients.

By providing valuable information and answering questions, real estate professionals can establish themselves as experts in their field and generate more leads. It also helps to stay updated with the latest trends in the real estate market.

## 34. OFFER FREE REAL ESTATE CONSULTATIONS IN YOUR FAVORITE COFFEE SHOP

Offering free real estate consultations in your favorite coffee shop is a simple and effective way to market your services as a real estate agent. This strategy can help you attract potential leads without the need for a lot of effort on your part.

One of the key benefits of this approach is that it allows you to connect with potential clients in a casual and relaxed setting. People enjoying their coffee are more likely to be open to a conversation and less likely to be guarded or skeptical. This makes it easier to start a conversation and build a relationship.

Another benefit of this approach is that it can be a cost-effective way to market your services. Advertising in traditional media can be expensive, and the results can be difficult to track. But by offering free consultations in a coffee shop, you can reach a targeted audience of people who are already interested in real estate. The coffee shop is a great place to showcase your knowledge of local neighborhoods and real estate trends.

When you're ready to offer consultations, simply place a sticker on your laptop or notebook that reads "Free Real Estate Advice." This can function as a free ad that other customers in the shop can see and can be a great way to attract potential leads.

You can also take it one step further and offer a complimentary coffee or pastry to anyone who agrees to a consultation. This gesture of goodwill will make the potential client feel appreciated and valued. This can help to establish a positive and personal connection.

You can also network with other local small business owners, such as the owner of the coffee shop, and ask them to spread the word among their customers. You can also leverage your social media accounts to let people know you offer free consultations. Set up a coffee shop and tag the coffee shop in your post. Surprisingly, this is a great tactic!

Offering free real estate consultations in your favorite coffee shop can be a simple and effective way to market your services as a real estate agent. It allows you to connect with potential clients in a relaxed setting, provides a cost-effective way of advertising, and helps you to showcase your knowledge of local neighborhoods and real estate trends. With a little effort, this strategy can help you attract new leads and build your business.

## 35. ACQUIRE MORE REFERRALS THROUGH LOCAL CONNECTIONS

Acquiring more referrals through local connections is essential for any realtor looking to grow their business. Referrals are one of the most effective ways to generate new leads, as they come from trusted sources and have a higher conversion rate. However, new agents may find it challenging to acquire referrals, which is where a strategic approach comes in.

One way to establish more local connections is by targeting a specific area. This allows you to focus your efforts on a specific geographic location, making it easier to build relationships and establish trust with potential clients. It also allows you to gain a deeper understanding of the local market and be able to provide valuable insights and advice to potential clients.

Another way to establish more local connections is by networking with local business owners. This could include other real estate professionals, mortgage brokers, home inspectors, and related service providers. By building relationships with these individuals, you can increase your visibility in the community, and they may also refer business to you. Below are a few ideas to get you started.

- Attend local networking events.
- Join the local chamber of commerce.
- Participate in local community events.

You can also leverage social media to build local connections. Platforms like Facebook and Instagram can be used to connect with potential clients in your target area by creating a local business page, sharing local market insights and updates, and participating in local community groups.

Acquiring more referrals through local connections is essential for any realtor looking to grow their business. A strategic approach, such as targeting a specific area, networking with other local business owners, and leveraging social media, can help establish more local connections and generate more referrals. Building relationships and establishing trust with potential clients can lead to more positive conversions and a steady stream of new leads.

## 36. BUY EXCLUSIVE SELLER LEADS

Buying exclusive seller leads is another shortcut for realtors to gain more leads for their business. Online platforms that sell leads can provide a wealth of information and data for real estate professionals. Making this a great way to find potential clients interested in selling their property. Additionally, these platforms often have exclusive deals for realtors based on zip code, which can help you target the most promising leads in your area.

One of the biggest benefits of buying exclusive seller leads is that they allow you to target potential clients already in the market to sell their property. This can be a great way to generate new leads, as these individuals are already actively looking for a realtor to help them with the selling process. Additionally, by purchasing leads at the start of the buyer's journey, you can be one of the first realtors to reach out to them and increase your chances of making a successful pitch.

Another benefit of buying exclusive seller leads is that they allow you to save time and effort compared to traditional lead generation methods. Instead of spending a lot of time and resources on generating leads, you can use the data provided by the platform. Use this data to target potential clients who are already interested in selling their property. This can free up your time and energy to focus on other important aspects of your business, such as closing deals and providing excellent customer service.

When purchasing exclusive seller leads, it is important to work with reputable platforms with a track record of providing high-quality leads. Researching and comparing different lead providers and reading reviews from other real estate professionals can help you find a platform that meets your needs. Additionally, check the quality of their leads by getting a sample of leads before making any big purchase. It can help you identify if the platform is providing you with high-quality leads or not.

Additionally, it's important to note that buying leads should not be the only strategy in your lead generation efforts. It should be a part of a well-rounded approach that includes other methods such as networking, marketing, and building relationships.

## 37. DISTRIBUTE YOUR BUSINESS CARDS AND SEASONAL TREATS

Distributing your business cards and seasonal treats is a great way for realtors to increase visibility and connect with potential clients. This strategy can be an effective way to generate new leads and is simple to execute. By taking advantage of seasonal events and special times of the day, you can increase your chances of reaching potential clients and making a lasting impression.

One of the most effective ways to distribute your business cards and seasonal treats is by handing them out during your daily activities. For example, why hand out a few cards to other shoppers if you are out buying your groceries? This can be a great way to connect with people who live or work near you and increase your visibility in the community. You can also hand out your cards to people you meet at the gym, at the park, or while doing other daily activities.

Another effective way to distribute your business cards and seasonal treats is by taking advantage of special times of the day, such as holidays. Holidays are a great time to connect with potential clients, as people are often festive and receptive. For example, you can give out water bottles or small treats that feature your business name and services offered during holidays like Halloween, Christmas, and Easter. This can be a great way to make a lasting impression on potential clients and increase your visibility in the community.

You can also take advantage of special events in your community to distribute your business cards and seasonal treats. For example, you can participate in local festivals, charity events, and community gatherings. This can help you connect with potential clients and increase your visibility in the community.

In addition to the distribution of your business cards and seasonal treats, you can also leverage the power of social media to increase your visibility. You can post pictures of your business cards and seasonal treats on your social media accounts and tag the location where you distributed them. This can help increase your visibility online and make potential clients more likely to come across your business.

## 38. GO KNOCKING ON DOORS

Door-to-door communication is a personal and direct way to connect with potential buyers and sellers. It allows realtors to build relationships, gain trust, and understand the specific needs of their clients. It is a simple yet powerful method that can significantly increase the chances of closing a deal.

One of the main advantages of door-to-door communication is that it allows realtors to reach a broader audience. Unlike digital marketing, which can target specific demographics, door-to-door communication allows realtors to connect with people of all ages, backgrounds, and income levels. This can be especially beneficial for realtors looking to expand their reach and attract new clients.

Another advantage of door-to-door communication is that it allows realtors to gather valuable information about the local market. By talking to homeowners and potential buyers, realtors can learn about the current state of the market and find out what people are looking for in a home. This information can be used to tailor their marketing efforts and create more effective marketing campaigns.

Realtors can also use door-to-door communication to build relationships with their clients. Realtors can gain trust and establish a personal connection with their clients by talking to people face-to-face. This can be especially important when working with first-time homebuyers who may be nervous or unsure about the buying process.

Door-to-door communication can be an effective way to generate leads. Realtors can identify potential sellers considering putting their homes on the market. Making this a great way to generate new listings and help realtors stay ahead of their competitors.

Furthermore, door-to-door communication is a powerful tool that can help realtors succeed in the digital age. Realtors can reach a broader audience, gather valuable information about the local market, build relationships with their clients, and generate leads. By incorporating door-to-door communication into their marketing strategy, realtors can increase their chances of closing deals and growing their businesses.

## 39. MAKE SOME OUTBOUND PHONE CALLS YOURSELF

Outbound phone calls can be an effective way for realtors to connect with potential clients and generate leads. By reaching out to people directly, realtors can quickly and easily establish a connection and learn more about the needs of their clients.

One of the main advantages of making outbound phone calls is that it allows realtors to reach a large number of people in a short amount of time. Unlike door-to-door communication, which can be time-consuming, outbound phone calls can be done quickly and efficiently. This can be especially beneficial for realtors looking to generate leads quickly and grow their business.

Another advantage of making outbound phone calls is that it allows realtors to gather valuable information about the local market. By talking to homeowners and potential buyers, realtors can learn about the current state of the market and find out what people are looking for in a home. This information can be used to tailor their marketing efforts and create more effective marketing campaigns.

Realtors can also use outbound phone calls to build relationships with their clients. Realtors can gain trust and establish a personal connection with their clients by talking to people over the phone. This can be especially important when working with first-time homebuyers who may be nervous or unsure about the buying process.

Outbound phone calls can also be an effective way to generate leads. Realtors can identify potential sellers who may be considering putting their home on the market by talking to homeowners. This can be a great way to generate new listings and help realtors stay ahead of their competitors.

Remembering that it's essential to have a script or an idea of what you want to say before making these calls. It can be easy to get flustered and lose track of what you want to say. A script will also help you stay on topic and make the most of your time on the call.

## 40. BE A COLD CALLING MASTER

Cold calling can be a powerful tool for realtors looking to generate leads and close deals. By actively reaching out to potential clients, realtors can establish a connection, learn more about the needs of their clients and position themselves as experts in their field.

One of the main advantages of cold calling is that it allows realtors to reach a broad audience. Unlike traditional forms of marketing, which can be targeted to specific demographics, cold calling allows realtors to connect with people of all ages, backgrounds, and income levels. This can be especially beneficial for realtors looking to expand their reach and attract new clients.

Another advantage of cold calling is that it allows realtors to gather valuable information about the local market. By talking to homeowners and potential buyers, realtors can learn about the current state of the market and find out what people are looking for in a home. This information can be used to tailor their marketing efforts and create more effective marketing campaigns.

Realtors can also use cold calling to build relationships with their clients. Realtors can gain trust and establish a personal connection with their clients by talking to people over the phone. This can be especially important when working with first-time homebuyers who may be nervous or unsure about the buying process.

Cold calling can also be an effective way to generate leads. Realtors can identify potential sellers considering putting their homes on the market by talking to homeowners. This can be a great way to generate new listings and help realtors stay ahead of their competitors.

One of the most significant challenges of cold calling is dealing with rejection. Rejection is a part of the process, and it's essential to have thick skin and be able to handle it. Remember that not every call will lead to a sale, but every call is an opportunity to learn and improve your skills.

## 41. TURN TO NEWS OUTLETS TO SHARE YOUR PITCH

Sharing your pitch to news outlets is an effective way for realtors to get their message in front of a large audience and generate leads. By reaching out to local news outlets, realtors can share their expertise, showcase their listings and position themselves as experts in their field.

One of the main advantages of sharing your pitch to news outlets is that it allows realtors to reach a broad audience. News outlets have a large audience and can help realtors to reach potential clients who may not be actively searching for a home. This can be especially beneficial for realtors looking to expand their reach and attract new clients.

Another advantage of sharing your pitch with news outlets is that it allows realtors to establish credibility and trust. Being featured in a news outlet allows realtors to showcase their expertise and establish themselves as a trusted authority in their field. This can be especially important when working with first-time homebuyers who may be nervous or unsure about the buying process.

Realtors can also use news outlets to showcase their listings and generate leads. By featuring their listings in a news outlet, realtors can reach a large audience and increase the chances of attracting potential buyers. This can be a great way to generate new leads and close deals.

When reaching out to news outlets, it's essential to have a clear and compelling pitch that highlights your expertise and showcases your listings. It's also important to be flexible and open to working with the news outlet to create content that will appeal to their audience.

Additionally, sharing your pitch to news outlets is an effective way for realtors to reach a broad audience, establish credibility and trust, and generate leads. By incorporating this strategy into their marketing efforts, realtors can increase their chances of closing deals and growing their businesses.

## 42. BE A PART OF THE LOCAL CHAMBER OF COMMERCE

Being a part of the local chamber of commerce is a great way for realtors to connect with other local business owners and generate leads. By becoming a chamber member, realtors can get their businesses listed on websites and newsletters, making it easier for potential clients to find them.

One of the main advantages of being a part of the local chamber of commerce is that it allows realtors to network with other local business owners. By participating in chamber events and meetings, realtors can make valuable connections and establish relationships with other business owners who can refer them to potential clients. This can be especially beneficial for realtors looking to expand their reach and attract new clients.

Another advantage of being a part of the local chamber of commerce is that it allows realtors to establish credibility and trust in the community. Realtors can showcase their commitment to the community by being chamber members and establishing themselves as a trusted authority in their field. This can be especially important when working with first-time homebuyers who may be nervous or unsure about the buying process.

Being a part of the local chamber of commerce can also be an effective way to generate leads. Realtors can connect with potential clients and showcase their listings by participating in chamber events and meetings. This can be a great way to generate new leads and close deals.

Participating in the local chamber of commerce is essential to be active and engaged. Attend events and meetings regularly, and take advantage of opportunities to network and connect with other business owners. Also, take the time to get to know the other members and build meaningful relationships.

In summary, being a part of the local chamber of commerce is a great way for realtors to connect with other local business owners, establish credibility and trust in the community, and generate leads. By incorporating this strategy into their marketing efforts, realtors can increase their chances of closing deals and growing their business.

## 43. STRATEGIZE YOUR HOLIDAY PLANS

While it's true that many people take holidays and vacations during the year, it's also true that many people are looking for homes during this time as well. In fact, the holiday season can be a great time to generate leads for your real estate business.

Here are a few strategies to consider:

1. **Host An Open House During The Holidays:** Many people are looking to move into a new home before the end of the year, and hosting an open house during the holidays can be a great way to generate leads.
2. **Create Holiday-Themed Marketing Materials:** Use the holiday season as an opportunity to create unique and eye-catching marketing materials that will help you stand out from your competition.
3. **Offer Special Deals Or Promotions:** Consider offering special deals or promotions to people looking to buy or sell a home during the holiday season. This can be a great way to generate leads and close deals.

4. **Attend Holiday Events:** Attend holiday events in your community and network with potential clients. This setting makes it easy to generate leads and build relationships with people looking to buy or sell a home.

5. **Target Expired Listings:** Expired listings are properties that have been on the market for a while but have yet to sell. The holiday season is a great time to reach out to these homeowners and offer your services.

6. **Target Out-Of-Town Buyers:** Many people relocate to new cities during the holidays, which can be a great opportunity to generate leads from out-of-town buyers.

7. **Partner With Local Businesses:** Partner with local businesses to offer special deals or promotions to their customers. This can be a great way to generate leads and build relationships with local businesses.

8. **Utilize Social Media:** Use social media platforms like Facebook, Instagram, and Twitter to reach out to potential clients and generate leads.

Realtors can use many different strategies to generate leads during the holiday season. Many different tactics can be effective, from hosting open houses to targeting expired listings. By thinking creatively and combining different strategies, you can generate leads and close deals during this special time of the year.

## 44. WATCH OUT FOR LEADS WITH COURT ORDERS

Court-ordered and divorce leads can be a great source of potential clients for realtors. These types of leads are often motivated to sell their property quickly, which can lead to faster closes and more successful deals. However, it's important to approach these leads with empathy and patience, as they may be going through a difficult time.

When it comes to court-ordered leads, it's important to understand the legal process and the court-order details. This can include researching the property's history, understanding any outstanding liens or judgments, and being familiar with the local court system. Additionally, it's important to be transparent with potential clients about the legal process and the potential risks and challenges involved in purchasing a court-ordered property.

Divorce leads can also be a valuable source of potential clients for realtors. These leads may be motivated to sell their property quickly to move on from their relationship and may also be willing to negotiate on price. However, it's important to approach these leads with empathy and understanding, as they may be going through a difficult and emotional time.

In addition to court-ordered and divorce leads, realtors should also focus on leads that want or need to move. This can include people relocating for work, families looking to upgrade or downgrade their living space, and investors looking to purchase rental properties.

Realtors should also consider using various marketing strategies to reach potential clients, including online and offline advertising, networking, and referral marketing. Social media platforms can be an excellent resource for reaching potential clients and traditional marketing methods such as flyers, brochures, and open houses.

Ultimately, it's important to remember that every lead is unique and may require a different approach. By being flexible, understanding, and transparent, realtors can close deals with court-ordered and divorce leads while also focusing on leads that want or need to move.

## 45. CONNECT AND NETWORK AT EVENTS NOT RELATED TO REAL ESTATE

Networking at events not directly related to real estate can be a great way for realtors to generate leads and build relationships with potential clients. By attending networking mixers, industry conferences, and community gatherings, realtors can connect with a wide variety of people in the market for a new home.

One key advantage of networking at events that are not directly related to real estate is that it allows realtors to reach potential clients who may not be actively searching for a new home. For example, by attending a networking event for small business owners, a realtor may connect with an entrepreneur looking to expand their business and move into a larger commercial space. By building relationships with these potential clients, realtors can be the first to know when they are ready to make a move.

Another advantage of networking at events not directly related to real estate is that it can help realtors establish themselves as experts in their field. By sharing their knowledge and experience with potential clients, realtors can position themselves as the go-to resource for all things real estate-related. This can be particularly useful for building trust and credibility with potential clients who may be hesitant to work with a realtor they have never met before.

When it comes to networking at events, it's important to be prepared and professional. This means having business cards, brochures, and any other marketing materials you may need to share with potential clients. It also means being prepared to talk about your business, services, and approach to working with clients. Additionally, it's important to be a good listener and ask questions to understand what potential clients are looking for in a home or investment property.

Networking at events that are not directly related to real estate can be a great way for realtors to generate leads and build relationships with potential clients. By attending various events, realtors can reach potential clients who may not be actively searching for a new home and position themselves as experts in their field. By being prepared, professional, and actively listening, realtors can make valuable connections that can lead to future business.

## 46. FORGE PARTNERSHIPS WITH LOCAL BRANDS

Partnering with local brands can be a great way for realtors to add value to their clients and generate leads. One example of this is partnering with a local furniture store. By working with a furniture store, a realtor can offer clients the opportunity to furnish their new home at a discounted rate or even for free. This can be a great way to differentiate yourself from other realtors and make the home buying or selling process more attractive to potential clients.

Another way to partner with local brands is to work with home staging companies. Home staging companies can help realtors make a property look its best when it is on the market. By working with a home staging company, a realtor can offer clients the opportunity to stage their homes at a discounted rate or even for free. The beauty of this strategy is that the property stands out from other properties on the market and makes it more attractive to potential buyers.

Another type of local brand you can partner with is interior design firms. Interior design firms can help realtors by providing their clients with design consultations and even full-service design projects. This can be a great way to add value to your clients and give them a more polished and finished product to sell.

Working with local home services companies such as cleaners, painters, landscapers, and handypersons can also greatly add value to your clients. By providing your clients with discounted or free services, you can help them prepare their property for sale or improve their new home for them.

Partnering with local brands can also help realtors generate leads. By working with a local furniture store, for example, a realtor can offer the store's customers a discounted rate on their services. Partnering can be a great way to reach new potential clients and generate leads.

Moreover, partnering with local brands can be a great way for realtors to add value to their clients and generate leads. Work with local furniture stores, home staging companies, interior design firms, and home service companies. By doing this, you can offer your clients a unique and valuable service, which will help them sell their property faster or improve their new home. Additionally, realtors can generate leads and expand their reach by offering free promotions to these local brands.

## 47. TARGET FSBOS

Targeting For Sale By Owners (FSBOs) can be a great way for realtors to generate leads and close deals. FSBOs are homeowners who are selling their property on their own without the help of a realtor. While these homeowners may be able to save money by not paying a realtor's commission, they may also need help navigating the complicated process of selling a home. By targeting FSBOs, realtors can offer their expertise and assistance while generating leads.

One way to target FSBOs is by searching for properties listed as "for sale by owner" on online real estate platforms such as Zillow and Realtor.com. Realtors can contact homeowners directly and offer their services by identifying these properties. It's important to remember that when approaching FSBOs, realtors should do so in a professional and non-threatening manner. This means respecting the homeowner's decision to sell their property independently and highlighting the benefits of working with a realtor without being pushy.

Another way to target FSBOs is by attending open houses for properties listed as "for sale by owner." This can be a great opportunity for realtors to meet homeowners in person and offer their services. Additionally, realtors can target FSBOs by searching for properties listed as "for sale by owner" in the newspaper or local classified ads.

It's also important to remember that while some FSBOs may be motivated by the desire to save money, others may have specific reasons for not wanting to work with a realtor. It's important to understand the motivations of the FSBOs and tailor your approach accordingly. For example, if a homeowner is motivated to save money, you can highlight how you can help them save money by negotiating a better sale price for the property. On the other hand, if the FSBO is motivated by a desire for control, you can highlight how you can help them navigate the process and take on some of the responsibilities that come with selling a home.

## 48. ONE-DAY LEASE

The decision to buy a house is one of the most significant transactions a person can make. Yet, many people make this decision almost blindly, needing to fully understand what it would be like to live in a particular home or neighborhood.

Realtors can address this issue and help potential buyers make more informed decisions by offering a "test day" program, similar to how a person can test drive a car before buying it.

The idea is simple: allow potential buyers to spend a day living in the home they are considering purchasing. Sounds crazy, I know! But here is how you do it! Set up the home as if it were lived in. Add furniture, decorations, and even food in the fridge. Potential buyers can then spend the day living in the home as they would if they were to purchase it, experiencing the layout, natural light, and overall feel of the space.

This type of program can be especially beneficial for out-of-town buyers who may have yet to have the opportunity to visit a property multiple times before making a decision. It can also be useful for buyers considering a major renovation or remodel, as they can see firsthand how the changes will affect the home's livability.

Another interesting idea is to create a "test weekend" program. This concept allows potential buyers to spend a weekend in the house, experiencing the neighborhood, the community, and the surrounding area. This can be done by providing them with a package that includes a guide to the best local restaurants, coffee shops, parks, and other points of interest.

In addition, you can use this program as a way to promote your properties. Create a website or social media platform where you feature the properties available for the test day or test weekend. Be sure to share pictures and videos of the experience, giving potential buyers a sense of what it would be like to live in the home.

Overall, offering a "test day" or "test weekend" program is a unique and innovative way for real estate professionals to help potential buyers make more informed decisions and ultimately close more deals. It allows potential buyers to experience a home in a way that simply viewing it cannot replicate, providing them with a sense of the property's livability and potential.

## 49. GIVE BACK TO YOUR LOCAL COMMUNITY

Giving back to your local community can be a great way for realtors to build relationships with potential clients and generate leads. By volunteering for nonprofit organizations or charities, realtors can demonstrate their commitment to the community and make a positive impact.

Realtors can give back to their local community by volunteering for a nonprofit or charity event. This can include working at a fundraising event, participating in a charity walk or run, or volunteering at a local food bank or homeless shelter. Realtors can meet and interact with potential clients by participating in these events while positively impacting their community.

Realtors can give back to their local community by organizing a charity event. This can include hosting a fundraiser, such as a silent auction or raffle, and donating a portion of the proceeds to a local nonprofit organization. By organizing an event, realtors can demonstrate their leadership skills and community spirit while raising awareness for a cause they care about.

In addition, realtors can also give back to the community by participating in local service projects, such as painting a community center or building a playground. These projects are a great way to get involved in the community and make a positive impact.

Realtors can demonstrate their commitment to the community and build relationships with potential clients by giving back to the community. Additionally, by participating in these activities, realtors can network with other community professionals, such as realtors, mortgage brokers, and home inspectors.

Furthermore, giving back to your local community can be a great way for realtors to build relationships with potential clients and generate leads. By volunteering for nonprofit organizations or charities, organizing charity events, or participating in local service projects, realtors can demonstrate their commitment to the community and make a positive impact.

These efforts can help realtors earn the trust of community members and entice them to choose you when they need or want to sell or buy a property.

## 50. GUERILLA MARKETING

Guerrilla marketing is a creative and unorthodox approach to marketing that can be highly effective for real estate professionals looking to increase sales and spark interest in their properties and services.

Realtors can use guerrilla marketing by creating unique and eye-catching property listings. For example, you can create a virtual reality tour of a property, a 3D walk-through of a property, or create a video that showcases the property in an interesting and unique way. By standing out from the competition, you can grab the attention of potential buyers and sellers and increase your chances of closing a deal.

Another approach is to create guerrilla marketing campaigns that target specific demographics or niches. For example, you can create a campaign focusing on first-time home buyers, luxury property buyers, or retirees. By targeting a specific demographic or niche, you can reach a highly targeted and engaged audience that is more likely to become a client.

Realtors can also use guerrilla marketing to host unique and creative events that showcase their properties and services. For example, you can host a rooftop party on a luxury property, an open house with a BBQ party, or a home staging workshop. Hosting unique, fun, and engaging events can attract potential buyers and sellers and create positive associations with your brand.

Using street teams, flash mobs, or stunts, you can also use guerrilla marketing to create a buzz around a new development or community. This approach can help create excitement and anticipation around a new property or development and can help attract more buyers and sellers.

Another interesting idea is to create a referral program where your current clients can refer you to their friends and family, and in return, they receive a monetary incentive. This can be a great way to generate more leads and create a sense of loyalty among your current clients.

In addition, you can use guerrilla marketing to boost your search engine optimization efforts by using local SEO techniques and publishing your properties on different platforms such as Zillow, Trulia, Redfin, and Realtor.com.

# CREATIVE ONLINE MARKETING IDEAS FOR REAL ESTATE AGENTS

## 51. GOOGLE MAPS MARKETING

Google Maps is a powerful and underutilized tool for real estate professionals looking to promote their properties and services. With the right approach, Google Maps can completely transform how you market real estate and help you reach a wider audience of potential buyers and sellers.

One way to use Google Maps for real estate marketing is by creating a Google My Business listing for your business. This will allow you to create a profile for your business that includes your contact information, hours of operation, and photos of your properties. It also allows potential buyers to see your location on the map and get directions to your office.

Another strategy is to create virtual tours of your properties using Google Street View. This can be done using Google's Street View app to take 360-degree photos of your properties and then publish them on your website and social media channels. Virtual tours can give potential buyers a sense of the layout and features of a property, even if they cannot visit it in person.

You can also use Google Maps to create custom maps that showcase your properties and the surrounding area. For example, you can create a map highlighting the best local schools, parks, shopping, and other points of interest. This can be a great way to promote your properties and their lifestyle.

Google Maps also allows you to use location-based marketing techniques. You can use the location data of your potential buyers to send them notifications and information about your properties nearby. This can be a great way to generate leads and drive traffic to your website.

In addition, you can use Google Maps to boost your search engine optimization efforts by optimizing your Google My Business listing and adding keywords and meta tags to your virtual tours and custom maps.

Overall, Google Maps is a powerful and underutilized tool for real estate professionals looking to promote their properties and services. With the right approach, Google Maps can help you reach a wider audience of potential buyers and sellers, generate leads, and, ultimately, close more deals.

## 52. ATTRACT LEADS FROM CRAIGSLIST

Craigslist is a powerful platform for real estate agents to generate qualified leads and reach potential buyers. The platform is free to use, making it an attractive option for agents looking to advertise their listings without spending much money.

You'll need to create a Craigslist account and post your listings to get started. Be sure to include high-quality photos, detailed descriptions, and your contact information. You can also post virtual tours, floor plans, and other relevant information to make your listings stand out.

One of the key advantages of using Craigslist is its immense popularity. The platform receives billions of visitors each month, making it an effective way to reach a large audience of potential buyers. Additionally, you can use Craigslist's search function to target your listings to specific demographics, such as location, price range, and property type.

Another advantage of using Craigslist is that you can post in multiple cities and regions. This can help increase your listings' visibility and reach potential buyers in different areas. Additionally, you can use Craigslist's advanced search function to target your listings to specific keywords, interests, and topics.

However, it's important to remember that you are not the only one posting on craigslist, so it's important to be creative and find ways to make your listings stand out. One way to do this is by using eye-catching headlines and descriptions that grab the reader's attention. Additionally, you can use social media to promote your listings and encourage potential buyers to check them out on Craigslist.

Try using Craigslist's built-in analytics to track the performance of your listings. This can help you identify which listings are performing well and which may need adjustments. Additionally, you can use this information to optimize your listings for better results.

## 53. USE LEAD GENERATORS

Lead generators, such as Realtor.com, Trulia, and Zillow, have become increasingly popular among real estate agents to generate leads and reach potential buyers. These websites allow agents to list their properties and reach a wider audience of potential buyers.

However, opinions on the effectiveness of lead generators vary among real estate agents, with some claiming they have helped them succeed and others finding them less effective.

One of the main advantages of lead generators is the reach they provide. Realtor.com, Trulia, and Zillow are among the most popular real estate websites, with millions of monthly visitors. This means that by listing your properties on these sites, you can reach a large audience of potential buyers who are actively searching for properties in your area. Additionally, many of these sites offer advanced search functions, which allow buyers to search for properties based on specific criteria, such as location, price range, and property type.

Another advantage of lead generators is the ability to track the performance of your listings. Many of these sites offer built-in analytics, which allows you to track the number of views, clicks, and leads generated by your listings. This can help you identify which listings are performing well and which may need adjustments. Additionally, these sites often provide insights on property views, leads, and other metrics that can help realtors to optimize their real estate advertising strategy.

However, it's important to keep in mind that lead generators can be highly competitive, with many real estate agents vying for the attention of potential buyers. Therefore, to be successful, it's important to use high-quality photos, detailed descriptions, and other relevant information to make your listings stand out.

Try using paid advertising on these sites to increase the visibility of your listings and reach a wider audience of potential buyers.

## 54. FOCUS ON BUILDING YOUR BRAND

Focusing on building your brand is a powerful way for realtors to generate leads and grow their business. A brand is people's perception of your business, formed by how people talk about your products and services. By building a strong brand, realtors can differentiate themselves from their competitors and establish themselves as a trusted and credible resource for potential clients.

One way to build your brand is by creating a strong online presence. Create a professional website, using social media platforms like Facebook, Instagram, and Twitter, and creating valuable and informative content such as blog posts, articles, and videos. By creating a strong online presence, realtors can establish themselves as experts in their field and build trust with potential clients.

Another way to build your brand is by creating a consistent visual identity. This includes creating a logo and color scheme and using them consistently across all your marketing materials, such as business cards, brochures, and flyers. This can help potential clients easily recognize your brand and remember you when they're ready to buy or sell a property.

In addition, realtors can also build their brand by networking with other industry professionals, such as realtors, mortgage brokers, and home inspectors. Realtors can establish themselves as trusted and credible resources by building relationships with these professionals and generating leads.

It's also important to focus on building a strong reputation. This can be done by providing excellent customer service, responding to customer complaints and feedback, and being responsive and communicative with your clients. By building a strong reputation, realtors can earn the trust of potential clients and generate leads through word-of-mouth marketing.

Focusing on building your brand is a powerful way for realtors to generate leads and grow their business.

## 55. GET MORE LOCAL LEADS WITH PREDICTIVE ANALYSIS

Predictive analysis is a powerful tool that can help realtors generate more local leads. Predictive analysis uses data, statistical algorithms, and machine learning techniques to identify the likelihood of future outcomes based on historical data. This can be particularly useful for realtors looking to generate leads in their local area.

One way to use predictive analytics for lead generation is by analyzing data on home sales in your local area. This can include data on home prices, sale dates, and property characteristics. Realtors can identify patterns and trends that can help them identify potential leads by analyzing this data.

For example, if a realtor knows that a particular neighborhood has a high number of homes selling in a certain price range, they can target their marketing efforts to that neighborhood and that price range to generate more leads.

Another way to use predictive analytics for lead generation is by analyzing data on consumer behavior in your local area. Include data on consumer demographics, lifestyle, and buying habits. Realtors can identify potential leads by analyzing this data and tailoring their marketing efforts to those consumers. For example, suppose a realtor knows a particular neighborhood is popular among young professionals. In that case, they can target their marketing efforts to that neighborhood and that demographic to generate more leads.

Additionally, some platforms and channels provide predictive analysis services to help realtors generate more leads. For example, some real estate websites and apps provide predictive analysis tools that help realtors identify potential leads based on the search criteria consumers use on their platform. This can include data on location, property type, and price range.

Predictive analysis can be a powerful tool for realtors looking to generate more local leads. Realtors can identify patterns and trends that can help them generate more leads by analyzing home sales and consumer behavior in their local area.

## 56. RANK ARTICLES FOR YOUR LISTINGS ON GOOGLE

Ranking articles for your listings on Google can be a powerful way for realtors to generate leads and attract more potential buyers to their properties. By targeting niche-specific keywords and using them in your articles, you can ensure that your properties are more easily found by potential buyers searching for properties in your area.

One way to rank articles for your listings on Google is by creating detailed and informative blog posts about your properties. These blog posts should include detailed information about the property, such as its location, size, and features, as well as high-quality images and videos of the property. Additionally, it's important to use niche-specific keywords in your blog post titles and throughout the content, as this can help your articles rank higher in search engine results pages (SERPs).

Another way to rank articles for your listings on Google is by creating detailed and informative articles about the local real estate market. These articles can include information about the local housing market, including data on home prices, sale dates, and property characteristics. By creating these articles, realtors can establish themselves as experts in the local real estate market, which can help them attract more potential buyers to their properties.

Don't forget that you can also use Google My Business and Maps to rank your listings on Google. You can create a business listing on Google My Business and include information about your business, such as your address, phone number, and website. Additionally, you can add photos and videos of your properties to your Google My Business listing to help potential buyers find your properties more easily.

Ranking articles for your listings on Google can be a powerful way for realtors to generate leads and attract more potential buyers to their properties. Create detailed and informative blog posts and articles about your properties. Include information about the local real estate market using niche-specific keywords.

Realtors can ensure that their properties are more easily found by potential buyers searching for properties in their area. Using Google My Business and Google Maps to boost your local SEO can also greatly increase leads.

## 57. CLAIM YOUR REAL ESTATE BUSINESS ON GOOGLE

Claiming your real estate business on Google can be a powerful way for realtors to generate leads and attract more potential clients. By creating a Google My Business account, realtors can ensure that their business is easily found by potential clients who are searching for real estate services in their area.

A Google My Business account allows businesses to manage their online presence across Google, including Search and Maps. By creating a business listing on Google My Business, realtors can include important information about their business, such as their business name, address, phone number, website, and hours of operation. Additionally, realtors can add photos and videos of their properties and customer reviews to help potential clients get a better sense of what their business has to offer.

When potential clients search for real estate services on Google, the Google My Business listings will appear on the right-hand side of the search results, making it easy for potential clients to find and contact your business. Google My Business listings also appear on Google Maps, making it easy for potential clients to find your business when searching for real estate services in their area.

Another benefit of claiming your real estate business on Google is the ability to track and manage customer reviews. By responding to customer reviews, you can show potential clients that you care about their satisfaction and are dedicated to providing excellent customer service. Positive customer reviews can also help boost your business's credibility and increase the likelihood of attracting new clients.

Claiming your real estate business on Google can be a powerful way for realtors to generate leads and attract more potential clients. By creating a Google My Business account and including important information about your business, realtors can mae it easy for potential clients to find and contact their business.

## 58. START AN EMAIL CAMPAIGN

Starting an email campaign can be a powerful tool for realtors looking to generate leads and grow their businesses. Email remains one of the best real estate marketing ideas for a good reason - it is a highly effective way to reach potential clients and generate leads.

One way to start an email campaign is by creating a list of potential clients. This can include past clients, leads that you've generated through other marketing efforts, and people who have expressed interest in your business. By creating a list of potential clients, you can ensure that your email campaign targets those most likely interested in your services.

Another way to start an email campaign is by creating a series of email templates that you can use to reach out to potential clients. These email templates should be visually appealing, easy to read, and include clear and concise information about your services. Additionally, it's important to include calls to action in your email templates, such as a link to your website or a phone number that potential clients can use to contact you.

Create a schedule for your email campaign; we urge you to use these tools to make life easier. This can include sending out regular emails, such as a weekly newsletter, or sending out targeted emails, such as an email to potential clients who have expressed interest in a specific property. By creating a schedule for your email campaign, you can ensure that you're reaching out to potential clients regularly, which can help increase the chances of generating leads.

## 59. LET PPC ADS WORK FOR YOU

PPC or pay-per-click advertising can be a powerful tool for realtors looking to generate leads and grow their business. When users search for specific keywords, PPC ads appear at the top of search engine results pages (SERPs). When done properly, PPC ads can effectively generate low-cost but high-quality leads for your real estate business.

One way to use PPC ads to generate leads is by targeting specific keywords that are relevant to your business. For example, if you're a realtor in a specific city, you might want to target keywords such as "homes for sale in [city name]" or "real estate listings in [city name]." By targeting these keywords, you can ensure that your ads are only being seen by users actively searching for properties in your area.

Another way to use PPC ads to generate leads is targeting specific demographics. For example, if you're a realtor who specializes in helping first-time home buyers, you could target your ads to users who are searching for homes in a specific price range or with certain features. By targeting specific demographics, you can ensure that your ads are only being seen by users who are most likely interested in your services.

You can also use PPC ads to generate leads using different formats such as Google Adwords, Bing Ads, Facebook Ads, and Instagram Ads.

## 60. ADD AFFILIATE MARKETING TO YOUR ARSENAL

Affiliate marketing is a powerful tool that can be used by real estate agents to earn additional income by recommending services or businesses of other people. This can include home inspection services, mortgage brokers, and even real estate agents. By partnering with other businesses, you can earn a commission on any sales that result from your referral.

One of the biggest advantages of affiliate marketing is that it can be done in addition to your regular business, allowing you to earn extra income without putting in extra work. This is especially beneficial for real estate agents who may already have a full schedule. Additionally, affiliate marketing can be done online, making it easy to reach a wider audience and generate more leads.

Another benefit of affiliate marketing is that it allows you to build relationships with other businesses and professionals in the industry. By working together, you can create mutually beneficial partnerships to help your businesses grow. This can be especially important for real estate agents who are looking to expand their network and build their brand.

Additionally, as an investor, you can use affiliate marketing to recommend your own services and products to others. This can include anything from investment properties to courses on investing in real estate. Doing this can increase your visibility and reach more potential investors.

To start with affiliate marketing, you will need to research and find businesses you can partner with. This can include home inspection services, mortgage brokers, and other real estate agents. Once you have identified a business with which you want to partner, you will need to reach out to them and negotiate a commission rate.

When promoting the services or products of your affiliate partners, it's important to be transparent with your audience. You should clearly disclose that you are earning a commission on any sales that result from your referral. Additionally, you should only recommend services or products you truly believe in and think will benefit your audience.

## 61. HARNESS THE POWER OF LOCAL ADS

Online advertising is a powerful tool that can be used by real estate agents to reach local homeowners and generate more leads. Local ads are a great way to target your advertising efforts to people in your area who are most likely to be interested in buying or selling a property. These ads can be placed on local news websites, social media platforms, or search engines like Google.

One of the biggest advantages of local ads is that they allow you to reach a highly targeted audience. By targeting your advertising efforts to people in your area, you are more likely to reach people actively looking to buy or sell a property. Additionally, local ads can be more cost-effective than other forms of advertising, as you are only paying for the people most likely to be interested in your services.

Another benefit of local ads is that they can help to establish your business as a trusted and reputable agent in your area. Regularly advertising in your local market can build brand awareness and create a sense of trust with potential clients. This can be especially important in the real estate industry, where clients need to trust their agent to make important decisions about buying or selling a property.

When creating local ads, you must consider your target audience and what they find valuable. This can include anything from advice on buying or selling a home to information on the local housing market. Additionally, you should ensure that your ad is visually appealing and easy to understand. You can also consider adding a call-to-action, such as a link to your website or a phone number, so potential clients can easily contact you.

To get started with local ads, you will need to research the different available platforms. This can include anything from local news websites to social media platforms like Facebook and Instagram. Once you have identified a platform you want to use, you will need to create your ad and set a budget for your advertising efforts.

## 62. POST A QUIZ

Posting a quiz is a fun and interactive way to pique the interest of potential buyers and boost your credibility as a real estate agent. Creating engaging and informative quizzes can increase your brand's engagement and generate more leads.

One of the biggest advantages of posting a quiz is that it allows you to gather valuable information about your audience. By asking questions about their housing needs and preferences, you can better understand what they are looking for in a property. This information can be used to tailor your marketing efforts and better target your audience.

Increase engagement with your brand. By creating fun and interactive quizzes, you can encourage people to share the quiz with their friends and family, which can help increase your reach and generate more leads. Additionally, quizzes can be shared on social media, which can help to increase your visibility and reach even more potential buyers.

When creating your quiz, it's important to consider your target audience and what they find valuable. This can include anything from questions about the local housing market to advice on buying or selling a home. Additionally, you should ensure that your quiz is visually appealing and easy to understand. You can also consider adding a call-to-action, such as a link to your website or a phone number, so potential clients can easily contact you.

To start posting a quiz, you can use online quiz makers such as Google Forms or Typeform. Once you have created your quiz, you can share it on your website or social media or even send it via email to your contact list.

Posting a quiz is a fun and interactive way to pique the interest of potential buyers and boost your credibility as a real estate agent. Creating engaging and informative quizzes can increase engagement with your brand, gather valuable information about your audience, and generate more leads. Additionally, quizzes can be shared on social media, which can help to increase your visibility and reach even more potential buyers.

## 63. ANSWER QUESTIONS ONLINE

Answering questions online is a great way for real estate agents to establish themselves as experts in their field and build trust with potential clients. You can demonstrate your expertise and establish yourself as a credible and authentic resource by providing helpful and informative answers to questions.

One of the biggest advantages of answering questions online is that it allows you to reach a wider audience. You can reach people who may not have otherwise found your website or social media pages by answering questions on platforms such as Quora, Yahoo Answers, or other forums. Additionally, by providing helpful answers, you can increase the likelihood that people will remember you and seek out your services in the future.

Another benefit of answering questions online is that it can help you establish yourself as an expert in your field. You can demonstrate your knowledge and expertise to potential clients by providing informative and well-researched answers. This can be especially important in the real estate industry, where clients need to trust their agent to make important decisions about buying or selling a property.

Additionally, you can also use Craigslist to answer questions. Craigslist is an online platform that allows you to post classified ads and can be a great way to reach potential buyers and sellers in your local area. You can establish yourself as a credible and authentic resource by posting ads that answer common questions about buying or selling a property.

To get started with answering questions online, you will need to research the different available platforms. This can include anything from Quora to forums specific to your niche. Once you have identified a platform you want to use, you can start answering questions and providing helpful information to potential clients.

When answering questions online, it's important to be authentic and provide helpful and informative answers. You should also include your contact information, such as your website or phone number, so potential clients can easily reach out to you.

## 64. SPONSOR A WEB POST AND SUBMIT A PRESS RELEASE

Sponsoring a web post is a great way to reach a wider audience and increase brand exposure for your real estate business. By partnering with a website or blog relevant to your target market, you can create a post that features your listings and provides valuable information for potential buyers. This can help build credibility and trust with your audience, ultimately leading to more sales.

When creating a sponsored web post, it's important to make sure that the content is high-quality and provides value to the reader. This could include local market trends, tips for buying or selling a property, or even a spotlight on a specific listing you are particularly excited about. The post should also include images and videos, as these are more likely to grab the reader's attention and keep them engaged.

In addition to sponsoring a web post, it's also a good idea to submit a press release to local news outlets. This can help increase your business's awareness and establish you as a respected and knowledgeable expert in the local real estate market. Press releases can also be used to announce new listings, share information about market trends, or highlight any awards or accolades your business has received.

When creating a press release, it's important to ensure that the information is accurate and newsworthy. The release should be concise and to the point and include a clear and compelling headline. It's also a good idea to include a quote from a representative of your business, as this can help to add a personal touch to the release and make it more appealing to readers.

Sponsoring a web post and submitting a press release can effectively increase brand exposure and establish credibility for your real estate business. It's important to ensure that the content is high-quality, provides value to the reader and that the press release is accurate and newsworthy. By combining these real estate marketing ideas, you can help to reach a wider audience and ultimately increase your chances of closing a sale.

## 65. MAKE THE MOST OF CRM TO SCALE YOUR LEAD GENERATION STRATEGY

A CRM, or customer relationship management system, is a powerful tool that can help realtors to scale their lead generation strategy and increase their chances of closing a sale. Using a CRM, realtors can easily manage and organize their leads, track their progress, and create customized campaigns tailored to each lead's needs and interests.

One of the key benefits of using a CRM for lead generation is that it allows realtors to automate many repetitive and time-consuming tasks associated with lead nurturing. This can include tasks such as sending follow-up emails, scheduling appointments and tracking leads as they move through the sales funnel. By automating these tasks, realtors can free up more time to focus on other important aspects of their business, such as building relationships with new leads and closing deals.

Another benefit of using a CRM for lead generation is that it can help realtors create targeted campaigns tailored to each individual lead's specific needs and interests. For example, a CRM can be used to segment leads based on factors such as demographics, location, or property type and then create customized campaigns that are tailored to each segment. This can help to increase the effectiveness of lead nurturing efforts and ultimately increase the chances of closing a sale.

Data privacy and security are the most important things to consider when using a CRM for lead generation. Ensure you comply with GDPR, HIPAA, and other data privacy regulations. You should also ensure that your CRM provider has robust security measures in place to protect your lead data from breaches and unauthorized access.

Using a CRM to scale your lead generation strategy can help you automate repetitive tasks and create targeted campaigns tailored to each individual lead's specific needs and interests. It can also help you keep your lead data organized and secure, ultimately leading to more sales and a more successful real estate business.

## 66. POST PROPERTY LISTINGS ON FACEBOOK MARKETPLACE

Posting your property listings on Facebook Marketplace can effectively reach a wider audience and increase your chances of closing a sale. With over 2 billion monthly active users, Facebook is one of the largest social media platforms in the world and can provide a valuable platform to showcase your listings.

When posting your property listings on Facebook Marketplace, it's important to make sure that you include all of the necessary details. This should include information such as the property's location, size, number of bedrooms and bathrooms, and any unique features or amenities. It's also important to include high-quality images and videos of the property, as these can help grab potential buyers' attention and provide them with a better sense of the property's layout and features.

One of the best ways to use Facebook Marketplace is to join local groups that are relevant to your target market. These groups are often named based on the area's name, and they provide a great way to connect with potential buyers in your local area. When joining these groups, it's important to read the group's policies and answer any questions they may have before getting accepted. Once you have joined the group, you can then start listing your properties.

You can also use the platform to connect with potential buyers and build relationships. This can include responding to comments and messages, sharing industry news and insights, and even hosting virtual tours or open houses. Building a relationship with potential buyers on Facebook can increase their trust in your brand and ultimately increase the chances of closing a sale.

Posting your property listings on Facebook Marketplace can effectively reach a wider audience and increase your chances of closing a sale. By joining local groups, providing all the necessary details, and including high-quality images and videos, you can showcase your listings in the best way possible.

Additionally, building relationships with potential buyers on the platform can increase their trust in your brand and ultimately increase the chances of closing a sale.

# UNIQUE AND CREATIVE IDEAS FOR REAL ESTATE MARKETING

## 67. HELP YOUR BUYERS FIND A GOOD INVESTMENT AND NOT JUST A HOUSE

As a realtor, it's important to not only help your buyers find a good house but also to help them find a good investment. By understanding your buyers' needs and goals, you can help them find properties that not only meet their immediate housing needs but also have the potential to appreciate in value over time.

One way to help buyers find a good investment is to work with accountants and business managers. These professionals can provide valuable insight into the financial aspects of real estate investing, such as cash flow analysis, rental income potential, and tax implications. They can also help buyers understand the benefits of investing in properties like single-family homes, duplexes, and multi-unit buildings.

Staying informed about the local real estate market is a great way to help clients. This can include keeping an eye on market trends, such as changes in home values, rental rates, and vacancy rates. By staying informed about the market, you can help buyers identify properties likely to appreciate in value over time.

When working with buyers, it's important to listen to their needs and goals and to be honest about the potential risks and rewards of different investment opportunities. By educating your buyers on the financial aspects of real estate investing and providing them with accurate and up-to-date information, you can help them make informed decisions and find properties that will be good investments for them.

You can also offer different services like property management, rental income estimation, and market analysis to help buyers understand the long-term benefits of owning a property. This can help to build a deeper relationship with buyers and give them more confidence in their purchase.

Helping your buyers find a good investment is an important aspect of being a realtor. By working with accountants and business managers and staying informed about the local market, you can help buyers understand the financial aspects of real estate investing and identify properties that have the potential to appreciate in value over time.

By providing additional services and educating buyers, you can help them make informed decisions and find properties that will be good investments for them.

## 68. PARTNER WITH A TRUSTED LOCAL HANDYMAN

Partnering with a trusted local handyman can be an invaluable resource for realtors. These expert professionals are often the first to hear about properties that are for sale or for rent, and they can provide valuable insights about the condition of a property, as well as potential upgrades, repairs, and renovations that may be needed. This can help realtors better understand prospective buyers' specific needs and provide them with more accurate and detailed information about a property.

Working with a handyman can also be a great way to attract buyers who are looking for a move-in-ready property. Realtors can help make the property more appealing to buyers and increase the chances of closing a sale by identifying and addressing any issues with a property before it goes on the market.

A handyman can provide a valuable service to sellers by helping them to prepare their property for sale. This can include helping sellers de- clutter, stage, and make minor repairs and renovations to their property, which can help make it more attractive to buyers. A handyman can also provide a useful resource for buyers looking to make changes or upgrades to a property after purchasing it.

When looking for a handyman to partner with, it's important to find someone who is reliable, professional, and has a good reputation in the local area. You can ask for references and check their online reviews to understand their work quality. Additionally, it's also important to ensure that the handyman is licensed and insured to protect yourself and your clients.

Partnering with a trusted local handyman can be a valuable resource for realtors. These expert professionals can provide valuable insights about a property and its condition and help prepare a property for sale. By working with a handyman, realtors can increase the chances of closing a sale and provide a valuable service to buyers and sellers. Make sure to do your due diligence when looking for a handyman to partner with and establish clear communication to ensure a smooth process.

## 69. CREATE AND ADVERTISE IN NEWSLETTERS

Creating and advertising in newsletters is an effective way for realtors to keep their previous clients and potential leads up to date with everything new in the real estate industry. Newsletters can be a great way to showcase new property listings, highlight company events, and provide valuable information about the local real estate market.

When creating a newsletter, it's important to ensure that the content is relevant and interesting to your target audience. This can include information about new property listings, market trends, and tips for buying or selling a property. It's also a good idea to include images and videos, as these can help to grab the reader's attention and make the newsletter more engaging.

You can also use your newsletter to showcase your company's achievements, such as new properties sold or bought, awards and accolades, and other notable milestones or events. This can help to establish your brand as a respected and successful player in the local real estate market.

In addition to creating a newsletter, it's also important to make sure that it reaches your target audience. This can include sending it out via email, sharing it on social media, or even mailing it to your current and potential clients. You can also consider promoting your newsletter on your website or other relevant platforms.

Another great way to increase your newsletter's reach is to partner with other local businesses and include their information in your newsletter. This can include information about local restaurants, events, and other relevant businesses to your target audience. This can help increase your newsletter's reach and establish you as a valuable resource in the local community.

Creating and advertising newsletters can be an effective way for realtors to keep their previous clients and potential leads up to date with everything new in the real estate industry. By ensuring that the content is relevant and interesting and that the newsletter reaches your target audience, you can establish your brand as a respected and successful player in the local real estate market. Partnering with other local businesses can also increase your newsletter's reach and establish you as a valuable resource in the local community.

## 70. LET AUTOMATED TEXT MARKETING DO THE WORK

Automated text marketing can be a powerful tool for realtors to reach potential leads and increase their chances of closing a sale. With an open rate of 97%, text messages have a significantly higher open rate than emails, making them an effective way to communicate with potential buyers and sellers. However, it's important to approach potential leads using text messages in a way that is professional, respectful, and compliant with laws and regulations.

When using automated text marketing, it's important to ensure that the messages are personalized and relevant to the recipient. This can include information about new listings, open houses, or other events that may interest the recipient. It's also important to make sure that the messages are timely and relevant, as sending irrelevant or outdated information can be off-putting to potential leads.

Automated text messaging can also be used for lead nurturing campaigns. You can set up automated text messages sent to leads at specific sales funnel stages, such as after a lead has shown interest in a particular property or after a lead has attended an open house. These messages can provide more information about the property, answer any questions the lead may have, or schedule a follow-up call or meeting.

Another important aspect of automated text messaging is ensuring you comply with laws and regulations. You should always obtain explicit consent from the recipient before sending text messages and include an opt-out option in every message. You should also ensure that you comply with TCPA (Telephone Consumer Protection Act) and other regulations.

Automated text marketing can be a powerful tool for realtors to reach potential leads and increase their chances of closing a sale. However, it's important to approach potential leads using text messages in a way that is professional, respectful, and compliant with laws and regulations.

If you want to take advantage of our done-for-you follow-up text messages, check https://soldouthouses.com/followup

# DIRECT REAL ESTATE
# MARKETING IDEAS

## 71. DISTRIBUTE LEAFLETS AND DOOR HANGERS

Leaflet and door hanger distribution is a tried and true real estate lead generation method. Not only does it allow you to share detailed information about your business and services, but it also allows you to target specific neighborhoods and demographics.

When creating your leaflets, include a clear and compelling call to action that encourages potential leads to contact you or visit your website. You can also include testimonials from previous clients and information about your certifications and awards.

To maximize the effectiveness of your leaflet distribution, choosing the right neighborhoods and demographics is important. Research the area you plan to distribute in and look for neighborhoods with a high concentration of homeowners. You can also target neighborhoods with a high turnover rate, as these likely have more potential leads.

Door hangers are another effective way to generate real estate leads, and they are a great way to capture the attention of potential leads not be actively looking to buy or sell a home. When creating your door hanger, include a clear, compelling message and a call to action that encourages potential leads to contact you or visit your website.

To maximize the effectiveness of your door-hanger distribution, choosing the right neighborhoods and demographics is important. Look for neighborhoods with a high concentration of homeowners and target neighborhoods with a high turnover rate. You can also target specific demographics, such as retirees or families with young children, who may be more likely to be in the market for a new home.

In addition to leaflet and door hanger distribution, consider other methods of lead generation such as online advertising, social media marketing, and networking. The key is to use various methods to reach potential leads and continuously monitor and adjust your strategy to ensure that it remains effective.

Overall, leaflet and door hanger distribution can effectively generate real estate leads, especially when targeted to the right neighborhoods and demographics. Realtors can increase their chances of attracting potential leads and growing their business by including a clear and compelling call-to-action and utilizing other lead-generation methods.

## 72. SEND YOUR SALE LETTERS TO ABSENTEE OWNERS

Sending sales letters to absentee owners is a great way for realtors to generate leads and grow their businesses. Absentee owners are individuals or companies that own a property but do not live or operate their business there. By targeting these individuals or companies, realtors can reach potential leads interested in selling or renting their property.

Direct and drip mail are the two main options for sending sales letters to absentee owners.

Direct mail refers to sending mail to select recipients. This method is more targeted and allows you to focus on specific individuals or companies more likely to be interested in your services. When using direct mail, it's important to research the properties and their owners before sending the letters. You can use online tools or public records to gather information about the properties and their owners.

Drip mail, on the other hand, is when you send out flyers or postcards to all the residents and contacts in your contact list or neighborhood. This method is less targeted, but it can be a good way to generate leads and build awareness about your business. When using drip mail, it's important to create visually appealing and professional-looking flyers or postcards that stand out and grab attention.

When creating your sales letters, include a clear and compelling message highlighting the benefits of working with you and your team. You can also include information about your certifications, awards, and testimonials from previous clients.

In addition to sending sales letters to absentee owners, consider other lead generation methods such as online advertising, social media marketing, and networking. The key is to use various methods to reach potential leads and continuously monitor and adjust your strategy to ensure that it remains effective.

Overall, sending sales letters to absentee owners can be an effective way for realtors to generate leads and grow their businesses. By targeting these individuals or companies and using a combination of direct and drip mail, realtors can increase their chances of attracting potential leads and closing more deals.

## 73. REACH OUT TO OWNERS OF EXPIRED OR OLD LISTINGS

Reaching out to owners of expired or old listings is a great way for realtors to generate leads and grow their business. Expired or old listings refer to properties that were once on the market but are no longer being actively marketed. By targeting these properties and their owners, realtors can reach potential leads who may be interested in selling or renting their properties.

When reaching out to expired or old listings owners, it's important to be respectful and understanding of their situation. Many of these owners may have had a negative experience with their previous realtor or personal circumstances that caused them to take their property off the market. By approaching them in a professional and understanding manner, you can build trust and establish a relationship with them.

When contacting the owners, you can ask if they are still interested in selling their property or if they have plans to put it back on the market. You can also use this opportunity to find out if they are aware of any issues that may have caused their property to expire or if they have any specific needs or concerns.

You can also use this chance to go through your list of buyers who might be more interested in older properties or those that might need some repair but are within their budget. By connecting these buyers with expired or old listings, you can help them find their dream home and also make a sale for themselves.

Consider other lead generation methods such as online advertising, social media marketing, and networking. The key is to use various methods to reach potential leads and continuously monitor and adjust your strategy to ensure that it remains effective.

Reaching out to owners of expired or old listings can be an effective way for realtors to generate leads and grow their business. By targeting these properties and their owners and connecting them with potential buyers, realtors can increase their chances of closing more deals and building their client base.

# FREE REAL ESTATE MARKETING IDEAS

## 74. ASK FOR REFERRALS AND OFFER INCENTIVES IN EXCHANGE.

Asking for referrals and offering incentives in exchange is a great way for realtors to generate leads and grow their businesses. Referrals are one of the most powerful forms of advertising. They come from people who have had a positive experience with your services and are willing to recommend you to others.

When asking for referrals, it's important to be direct and clear about what you're looking for. Feel free to reach out to your family, friends, coworkers, and existing clients. You can also offer incentives for referrals, such as discounts or gift cards, to encourage people to recommend your services.

When reaching out to potential referral sources, it's important to be respectful and professional. Please explain what you're looking for and how their referral can help you. You can also share information about your business and services and highlight any certifications or awards you have received.

When following up with referrals, it's essential to be prompt, professional, and respectful. Follow up with them as soon as possible, and be sure to thank them for the referral. Also, keep your referral sources in the loop on the referral's progress and let them know how it turns out.

In addition to asking for referrals, consider other lead-generation methods such as online advertising, social media marketing, and networking. The key is to use various methods to reach potential leads and continuously monitor and adjust your strategy to ensure that it remains effective.

Asking for referrals and offering incentives in exchange is a great way for realtors to generate leads and grow their business. You can tap into your network and offer incentives; realtors can increase their chances of attracting potential leads and closing more deals.

## 75. SHOW UP AT GARAGE SALES

Showing up at garage sales is a great way for realtors to generate leads and grow their business. Garage sales are a great way to meet potential leads in person and learn more about their needs and interests.

When showing up at garage sales, being professional and respectful is important. Dress professionally, bring business cards and other marketing materials, and be prepared to discuss your business and services.

It's also important to have a strategy in place for how you will approach potential leads. One effective strategy is to ask about the property they are selling and if they are interested in buying or selling any other properties. You can also ask if they know anyone looking to buy or sell a property or if they are interested in learning more about your services.

Another strategy is to take advantage of the opportunity to connect with potential buyers. You can ask them what they are looking for in a property and if they would be interested in receiving information about properties that match their criteria.

When leaving the garage sale, follow up with your leads as soon as possible. This can be through a phone call, email, or text message, and be sure to thank them for their time.

In addition to showing up at garage sales, consider other lead-generation methods such as online advertising, social media marketing, and networking. The key is to use various methods to reach potential leads and continuously monitor and adjust your strategy to ensure that it remains effective.

Overall, showing up at garage sales can be an effective way for realtors to generate leads and grow their business. By interacting with potential leads in person and having a strategy in place, realtors can increase their chances of attracting potential leads and closing more deals.

## 76. SHARE TESTIMONIALS

Sharing testimonials is a great way for realtors to generate leads and grow their business. Testimonials are powerful because they come from previous clients who have had a positive experience with your services. They can help build trust and credibility with potential leads and serve as an endorsement for your business.

When sharing testimonials, it's important to be selective and choose the most powerful and relevant testimonials. These should be from clients who have had a positive experience with your services and can speak to the specific benefits of working with you.

There are several ways to share testimonials. You can include them on your website, marketing materials, and social media. You can also use them in your email marketing campaigns and online advertising.

When using testimonials, include the client's name and a photo. When associating a name with a face, it becomes more believable. Testimonials allow potential leads to connect with them and ask them more about their experience.

Another way to share testimonials is to use video testimonials. This is a great way to showcase your clients' experiences and to provide potential leads with a more personal connection to your business.

In addition to sharing testimonials, consider other lead-generation methods such as online advertising, social media marketing, and networking. The key is to use various methods to reach potential leads and continuously monitor and adjust your strategy to ensure that it remains effective.

Sharing testimonials is a great way for realtors to generate leads and grow their business. By sharing positive feedback from previous clients, realtors can build trust and credibility with potential leads and increase their chances of closing more deals.

## 77. PROVIDE TOP-NOTCH CUSTOMER SERVICE

Providing top-notch customer service is crucial for realtors to generate leads and grow their businesses. Not only does it help to retain current clients, but it also generates new leads through positive word-of-mouth and referrals.

To provide top-notch customer service, building strong relationships with your clients is important. This can be done by being responsive and easy to reach, professional and respectful, and proactive in addressing any concerns or issues that may arise.

It's also important to be knowledgeable and well-informed about the market and the properties you are listing. This will help you to be better equipped to answer any questions your clients may have and to provide them with accurate and useful information.

Another way to provide top-notch customer service is by going above and beyond for your clients. This can be done by providing additional services such as home staging or by offering discounts on home inspection services. It can also be by providing your clients with detailed market analysis reports and other valuable resources.

In addition to providing top-notch customer service, consider other lead-generation methods such as online advertising, social media marketing, and networking. The key is to use various methods to reach potential leads and continuously monitor and adjust your strategy to ensure that it remains effective.

Overall, providing top-notch customer service is essential for realtors to generate leads and grow their businesses. By building strong relationships with clients and going above and beyond, realtors can increase their chances of retaining current clients and attracting new leads through positive word-of-mouth and referrals.

## 78. CREATE A REAL ESTATE FACEBOOK GROUP IN YOUR LOCAL AREA

Creating a real estate Facebook group in your local area is a great way for realtors to generate leads and grow their business. Using this Facebook group, you can connect with potential leads and offer them valuable information about buying and selling properties and other real estate-related topics.

When creating your Facebook group, be sure to choose a name that is relevant and easy to remember. You can include a brief description of the group and its purpose, along with the types of information that will be shared.

Encourage all your members to raise their questions about buying and selling properties and other inquiries they may have. This will help create an active community where potential leads can learn more about real estate and connect with like-minded individuals.

You can also post exclusive real estate tricks and tips, as well as real estate news and updates in the group. This will help to keep your members engaged and interested in the group.

If you have any free resources, such as an e-book or course about real estate, you can also promote them in the group. This will allow potential leads to learn more about your business and see the value that you can provide.

In addition to creating a real estate Facebook group, consider other lead generation methods such as online advertising, social media marketing, and networking. The key is to use various methods to reach potential leads and continuously monitor and adjust your strategy to ensure it remains effective.

Creating a real estate Facebook group in your local area is a great way for realtors to generate leads and grow their business. By connecting with potential leads and offering them valuable information and resources, realtors can increase their chances of attracting potential leads and closing more deals.

## 79. CREATE A CLIENT AVATAR FOR EASIER TARGETING IN SOCIAL MEDIA

Creating a client avatar is a great way for realtors to generate leads and grow their business by targeting their ideal clients on social media. A client avatar is a detailed representation of your ideal client, including their age, personality, family, needs, interests, and preferences. By understanding your ideal client, you can create and post content on social media specifically tailored to them, increasing the chances of attracting them to your business.

When creating your client avatar, consider the following details:

- Demographics: Age, gender, income, education level, and occupation
- Personality: Are they outgoing or introverted? Are they detail-oriented or big-picture thinkers?
- Family: Are they married or single? Do they have children, or are they planning to have children?
- Needs: What are their needs and priorities when it comes to buying or selling a property?
- Interests: What are their hobbies and interests?
- Preferences: What type of property do they prefer? What is their preferred location?

Once you clearly understand your ideal client, you can create and post content on social media specifically tailored to them. For example, suppose your ideal client is a young family looking for a starter home. In that case, you can create and post videos and blogs about family-friendly neighborhoods and properties suitable for children.

You can also use your client avatar to target your advertising on social media platforms. For example, suppose your ideal client is a retiree looking for a retirement home. In that case, you can target your advertising to individuals over the age of 55 with interests in retirement communities and properties.

## 80. START A CONTEST

Starting a contest is a great way for realtors to generate leads and grow their business by luring potential leads to a certain property listing. Contests are an easy and effective way to create buzz and excitement around your property listings and to encourage potential leads to take action.

When starting a contest, choosing a prize that will entice potential leads to put in their offers and close is important. Some great prizes include VIP tickets to a popular sporting event or concert, a new TV for their new house, a home appliance package, or a vacation package.

It's also important to ensure that the contest's rules are clear, easy to understand and follow. Be sure to include information about how to enter the contest, how the winner will be selected, and when the contest will end.

Another way to make the contest more interesting is by making it a referral contest. This can be done by rewarding the person who refers the most people to your contest with an extra prize.

To promote the contest, you can use various marketing channels such as social media, email marketing, and online advertising.

In addition to starting a contest, consider other lead-generation methods such as online advertising, social media marketing, and networking. The key is to use various methods to reach potential leads and continuously monitor and adjust your strategy to ensure that it remains effective.

Starting a contest is a great way for realtors to generate leads and grow their business. Realtors can increase their chances of attracting potential leads and closing more deals when they create buzz. Adding excitement around your property listings and offering incentives will entice potential leads to put in their offers and close them.

# REAL ESTATE ADVERTISING STRATEGIES USING ONLINE TOOLS

## 81. PUT ADS IN ONLINE NEWSPAPERS

Online newspaper ads are a valuable tool for realtors because they can reach a large local audience actively seeking information about real estate. This audience is often highly engaged and ready to take action, making it a great way to generate quality leads.

One of the biggest advantages of online newspaper ads is their ability to target a specific geographic area. This is particularly useful for realtors who specialize in a certain neighborhood or region. By advertising in a local newspaper, realtors can reach potential buyers and sellers who are specifically looking for properties in that area.

Another advantage of online newspaper ads is their cost-effectiveness. Online newspaper ads are relatively inexpensive compared to other forms of advertising, such as TV or radio. This means that realtors can reach a large audience without breaking the bank. Additionally, many online newspapers offer a range of ad formats and sizes, which can be customized to fit any budget.

Online newspaper ads are also a great way to build brand awareness. By consistently advertising in a local newspaper, realtors can establish themselves as a trusted and reputable source of real estate information in their community. This can lead to more word-of-mouth referrals and repeat business.

In addition to traditional online newspaper ads, many newspapers offer additional online marketing services to realtors, such as online classifieds, online property listings, and online open houses. These services can provide even more opportunities to connect with potential buyers and sellers.

Overall, online newspaper ads continue to provide value to realtors even in the modern digital age. Realtors can reach a targeted audience by looking for a trusted local newspaper, generating quality leads, and building brand awareness at an affordable cost.

## 82. AUTOMATE YOUR EMAIL MARKETING CAMPAIGNS

Email marketing is essential for realtors to stay in touch with clients and prospect leads. However, manually creating, sending, and tracking emails can be time-consuming and overwhelming. Automating your email marketing campaigns can simplify the process and make your life as a realtor much more convenient.

One of the main benefits of automating your email marketing campaigns is saving time. Instead of manually creating and sending emails, you can set up automated email sequences that will go out to your contacts at specific intervals. This can free up time for you to focus on other aspects of your business. You can also use automated email campaigns to nurture leads by sending targeted and relevant content to different groups of contacts based on their level of engagement with your brand.

Another benefit of automating your email marketing campaigns is that it increases efficiency. With automated emails, you can ensure that your contacts are receiving timely and relevant information. Additionally, automation tools like Mailchimp allow you to easily track the success of your email campaigns, including open rates, click-through rates, and conversions. This data can be used to optimize your campaigns and make them even more effective.

Automating your email marketing campaigns also allows you to personalize the content of your emails to make them more relevant to your contacts. You can segment your contact list based on demographics, location, and other factors and send tailored messages to different groups of contacts. Doing this increases their chances of engaging with your content and ultimately becoming your clients.

Moreover, Automation also allows you to schedule your emails in advance. Ensure your emails are sent at the most optimal time. This will increase the chances of your emails being opened and read.

If you want to get access to our done-for-you email marketing system & website, please visit

https://soldouthouses.com/easyfunnel/

## 83. DON'T LEAVE OUT YOUR EMAIL SIGNATURE

An email signature is a small but powerful tool that can greatly enhance a realtor's professional image and make it easier for clients and prospects to reach you. It's a simple way to make a lasting impression and ensure that your name and contact information is easily accessible to those who receive your emails.

Your email signature should be simple and informative, including your name, company name, and job title. It should also include your contact information, such as your cell and office numbers, and include all email addresses. Including a link to your website makes it easy for people to find more information about you and your services.

In addition to the basic contact information, you can include your social media profiles in your email signature. This can be a great way to personally connect with clients and prospects and stay top-of-mind. Social media platforms such as LinkedIn and Instagram can be great ways to showcase your listings and build your personal brand.

Another important aspect of an email signature is its design. A well-designed email signature can make a professional impression and set you apart from your competition. It's important to keep in mind that your email signature should match your company's branding and style. It should be consistent with your website, business cards, and other marketing materials.

When creating your email signature, it's important to consider the size and file type. It should be small enough to not cause any delays in sending or receiving emails but also large enough to be easily readable. It's best to use JPG or PNG file format as they are widely supported and maintain the quality of the image.

Your email signature is a powerful tool that can help realtors make a lasting impression and stay top-of-mind with clients and prospects. It should be simple yet informative, including pertinent contact information and a link to your website. You can also include your social media profiles to personally connect with clients and prospects. A well-designed email signature that matches your company's branding and style can set you apart from the competition.

## 84. HARNESS THE POWER OF FLIPBOOKS

Flipbooks are a great way to make your real estate presentations and brochures more interesting and attractive. They are an interactive way to showcase your listings and can help to make a lasting impression on potential buyers and sellers.

Creating a flipbook is easy and straightforward. There are many online tools available that can help you convert your existing PDFs or PowerPoints into flipbooks. These tools typically offer a variety of templates and customization options, allowing you to create flipbooks that match your branding and style.

One of the biggest advantages of flipbooks is their shareability. They can be easily shared via email or social media and embedded on your website. This allows you to reach a wider audience and increase your chances of generating leads. Additionally, since flipbooks can be easily shared, you can use them as a lead-generation tool. For example, you can embed a form within your flipbook that visitors can fill out to request more information or schedule a showing.

Flipbooks also look great and are much more engaging than traditional static brochures. They allow you to add interactive elements such as videos, images, and hyperlinks, making them more interactive and dynamic. This can help to keep potential buyers and sellers engaged and interested in your listings.

Another advantage of flipbooks is their accessibility. They can be easily viewed on any device, including desktop computers, laptops, tablets, and smartphones. This means that potential buyers and sellers can access your listings from anywhere, making it more convenient for them to learn about your properties.

Trying to turn your real estate presentations and brochures into flipbooks is a great way to make them more interesting and attractive. They are easy to make, shareable, and look great. They also offer many advantages over traditional static brochures, such as increased engagement, shareability, and accessibility. Using flipbooks, realtors can increase the chances of generating leads and closing more sales.

## 85. TRY GOOGLE ADS

Google Ads is a powerful tool for realtors looking to start their PPC advertising campaigns. As the world's most widely used search engine, Google can help realtors reach a large audience of potential buyers and sellers. With Google Ads, realtors can create targeted and effective ads that will appear at the top of search results, increasing the chances of being seen by potential clients.

One of the biggest advantages of Google Ads is its targeting capabilities. Real estate professionals can target specific geographic areas, demographics, and even specific keywords related to their listings. Doing this allows them to reach the right audience at the right time, increasing the chances of generating leads and closing sales.

Google Ads also provides realtors with a lot of data to analyze and optimize their campaigns. This can help them identify which ads are performing well and which need to be tweaked. Realtors can make informed decisions about how to improve their campaigns and get the best results by analyzing data such as click-through rates, conversion rates, and cost per click.

Another advantage of Google Ads is the ability to create different types of ads, such as text ads, display ads, and video ads. Text ads are the most common type of ad and are typically used to promote specific listings or services. Display ads are image-based ads used to showcase properties. Video ads allow realtors to create engaging videos showcasing the best of the property.

Additionally, Google Ads can target specific audiences, such as people who have recently searched for real estate-related keywords or have visited your website. This allows you to reach the most relevant audience and increase the chances of converting leads into clients.

Google Ads is a powerful tool that can help realtors reach a large audience of potential buyers and sellers. With its targeting capabilities, data analysis, and different types of ads, realtors can create targeted and effective ads. Ads that will appear at the top of search results, increasing the chances of being seen by potential clients. Real estate professionals can get the best results for their PPC advertising campaigns by utilizing Google Ads.

## 86. RESPOND QUICKLY AND INFORMATIVELY

As a realtor, responding quickly to queries is crucial to the success of your business. Potential buyers and sellers often have urgent questions or need to schedule viewings. A slow response can cause them to move on to another agent. Ensure that you are always available to your clients; it's important to have constant access to your email.

One of the easiest ways to achieve this is by setting up your email on your smartphone. Allowing you to receive and respond to emails on the go. Whether at a showing, meeting with clients or out of the office. Many smartphones also have push notifications, alerting you when you receive a new email and ensuring you never miss an important message.

Having your email set up on your smartphone allows you to easily access other important tools, such as your calendar, contacts, and notes. This makes it easy to schedule viewings, follow up with leads, and keep track of important details from one device.

Another advantage of having your email set up on your smartphone is the ability to easily access your email while out of the office. Responding to clients' queries, schedule viewings, and follow up on leads, even when you're not at your desk, is vital to success. This can help you stay connected to your clients and increase your chances of closing a sale.

To ensure you stay organized, it's important to set up your email on your smartphone in a way that makes it easy to manage.

- Set up filters
- Add labels
- Create folders
- Use a productivity app to help you keep track of your to-do list and schedule.

As a realtor, responding quickly to queries is crucial to the success of your business. This can help you stay connected to your clients, schedule viewings, and follow up on leads, even when you're out of the office. By staying organized, you can also ensure you can manage your emails efficiently and effectively.

## 87. DON'T FORGET TO RETARGET

Retargeting is a powerful marketing strategy that can help realtors leverage the window of opportunity that occurs between when a potential buyer or seller first starts researching properties and when they make a final decision. On average, it takes most people between two weeks to four months of research before they decide on what property to buy. Retargeting allows realtors to stay top-of-mind with potential clients during this crucial period.

Retargeting works by tracking a potential client's online behavior and then displaying targeted ads to them based on their interests and search history. For example, if a potential buyer visits a property listing on your website, a retargeting ad for that specific listing can be displayed to them as they continue to browse the internet. This helps to keep the property top-of-mind and increases the chances of them reaching out to schedule a viewing or request more information.

Retargeting is used to target specific demographics and geographic areas. For example, suppose you have a property listing in a specific area. In that case, you can use retargeting to target potential buyers or sellers who have recently searched for properties in that area. This can increase the chances of reaching the right audience and generating leads.

Retargeting can also be used to target specific stages of the buyer's journey. For example, you can use retargeting to target people who have recently viewed a property and are in the early stages of research. Or who have shown interest in a property and are in the final stages of decision-making. This allows you to tailor your marketing messages to specific audience segments and increase the chances of converting leads into clients.

Additionally, retargeting is a powerful marketing strategy that can help realtors leverage the window of opportunity that occurs between when a potential buyer or seller first starts researching properties and when they make a final decision.

It allows realtors to stay top-of-mind with potential clients, targets specific demographics and geographic areas, and tailor marketing messages to specific audience segments. Using retargeting, realtors can increase the chances of generating leads and closing more sales.

## 88. COME UP WITH SMART LISTING DESCRIPTIONS

As a realtor, standing out from the competition is essential to attract potential buyers and sellers to your listings. One way to do this is by using clever writing in your advertising efforts. A well-written ad can grab buyers' attention and create an emotional connection with them, making them more likely to schedule a viewing or consider your services.

One strategy for using clever writing is to focus on the property's unique selling points and use descriptive language to paint a picture of the property in the buyer's mind. This can be done by highlighting the property's best features, such as the view, the location, the layout, the finishes, etc. Also, you can use storytelling and descriptive language to create an emotional connection with the potential buyers and make them feel like they already live in the property.

Another strategy is storytelling to create an emotional connection with potential buyers. For example, you can use a story to highlight the benefits of the property. Such as the perfect backyard for hosting summer barbecues or the open floor plan is ideal for entertaining.

This can help to create a mental image of the property in the buyer's mind and make them more interested in scheduling a viewing.

Another way to use clever writing in your advertising efforts is by creating a sense of urgency. For example, instead of saying "for sale," you can say, "don't miss out on this rare opportunity." This can create a sense of excitement and encourage buyers to take action.

It's also important to use clever writing in your property descriptions, brochures, flyers, and other materials. Instead of generic terms, use descriptive language that paints a picture of the property.

For example, instead of saying, "the kitchen has granite countertops," you can say, "the kitchen boasts gleaming granite countertops that shine under the natural light." This can create a more vivid image of the property and make it more appealing to potential buyers.

Another tip is to use humor in your writing. Humor can help to make the property more relatable and memorable to the buyers. It can also help to show personality and make the realtor stand out from the rest.

## 89. MAKE THE MOST OUT OF YOUTUBE ADS

YouTube is a powerful platform for real estate agents to showcase their listings and reach potential buyers. One way to maximize the impact of your video listings is by incorporating them into a YouTube advertising campaign. By targeting your ads to a specific audience, you can ensure that your ads reach the most relevant and interested viewers.

To start, ensure your YouTube channel is up to date and optimized for search. This means using relevant keywords in your channel name, description, and video titles.

Additionally, make sure that your videos are high-quality, well-lit, and professionally edited. This will help to ensure that your ads stand out and catch the attention of potential buyers.

Once your YouTube channel is set up, you can create your ad campaign. You can use a variety of ad formats, such as skippable in-stream ads, non-skippable in-stream ads, and bumper ads. These ads can target specific demographics, such as age, gender, and location. By targeting your ads to viewers in your local area or city, you can ensure that your ads reach the most relevant and interested viewers.

To further increase the effectiveness of your ads, consider using call-to-action overlays or end screens on your videos. This can encourage viewers to take action, such as visiting your website or contacting you for more information. Additionally, you can use remarketing to target viewers who have previously engaged with your content. This can help to increase the likelihood that they will take action and contact you about a listing.

In addition to targeting viewers in your local area or city, you can also target specific keywords, interests, and topics to reach potential buyers who are actively searching for properties in your area. This can help increase your listings' visibility and reach a wider audience of potential buyers.

Incorporating your video listings into a YouTube advertising campaign greatly increases their visibility and reaches potential buyers. By targeting your ads to viewers in your local area or city, you can ensure that your ads reach the most relevant and interested viewers.

Additionally, using call-to-action overlays and remarketing can help increase your ads' effectiveness and encourage viewers to take action.

# STAY ACTIVE FOR BETTER REAL ESTATE ADVERTISING

## 90. ATTEND EVENTS RELATED TO REAL ESTATE

Attending trade shows and networking events is essential to building a successful real estate career. These events provide an excellent opportunity for realtors to meet and connect with industry leaders, potential clients, and other professionals in the field. They also offer a chance to learn about new trends and technologies and stay up-to-date on the latest developments in the industry.

One of the main benefits of attending trade shows is networking with other professionals in the field. These events are typically attended by a wide range of people, including real estate agents, brokers, developers, investors, and other industry leaders. Meeting and connecting with these individuals can build valuable relationships to help you grow your business. Additionally, you can stay in touch with these people after the event by exchanging business cards and contact information.

Trade shows also offer a great opportunity to learn about new trends and technologies in the real estate industry. Many of these events feature workshops, seminars, and panel discussions on various topics, from the latest marketing strategies to technological advances. By attending these sessions, you can gain valuable insights into the latest trends and best practices in the industry, which can help you stay competitive and successful in your business.

Another key benefit of attending trade shows is the ability to showcase your listings and services. Many trade shows feature exhibitor booths where realtors can display their listings and promote their services. This is an excellent opportunity to attract new clients and build your brand. Additionally, by handing out brochures and other marketing materials, you can reach a wider audience and generate more leads for your business.

Networking events also offer similar benefits as trade shows. Professional groups like the National Association of Realtors usually organize real estate networking events. They are designed specifically for real estate professionals. They are typically smaller and more focused than trade shows. They offer a more intimate setting for networking and building relationships.

## 91. JOIN HANDS WITH REAL ESTATE ONLINE BROKERAGES

Joining online brokerage platforms can be a valuable strategy for realtors looking to grow their businesses. These platforms connect realtors with a larger pool of potential clients and provide a range of tools and resources to help them succeed.

One of the main benefits of working with online brokerage platforms is receiving more qualified leads. These platforms typically have a large pool of potential buyers and sellers actively looking for real estate services. By joining these platforms, you will have access to this pool of leads and will be able to reach a wider audience of potential clients. Many of these platforms have advanced filtering and search capabilities. This allows you to target specific demographics and locations and increase your chances of finding the right clients for your business.

Another benefit of working with online brokerage platforms is that they provide a range of tools and resources to help you grow your business. Many platforms offer marketing and advertising services, such as email campaigns and social media management. These can help you reach a wider audience and generate more leads. Additionally, many of these platforms provide training and education, such as webinars and seminars, which can help you stay up-to-date on the latest trends and best practices in the industry.

Working with online brokerage platforms can also help you establish a strong online presence, which is essential in today's digital age. Many of these platforms have a website and mobile app that allow potential clients to search for properties and connect with agents. Additionally, many of these platforms provide tools to help you optimize your online listings, such as professional-grade photography and virtual tours.

It's important to note that some online brokerage platforms may require a monthly or annual fee to access their leads and tools. It's important to research the different platforms and their pricing options to find the one that best meets your needs and budget. Also, make sure to understand the terms of the agreement, such as the commission split, marketing expenses, and any other restrictions, before signing up.

## 92. CREATE PROFESSIONAL BUSINESS CARDS

Professional business cards are a simple but effective form of real estate advertising that every realtor should always have in their pocket. By keeping them handy, you can easily distribute them to potential clients, business partners, and other industry professionals whenever the opportunity arises.

One of the main benefits of professional business cards is that they provide a quick and easy way for potential clients to contact you.

What to include:

- Your name
- Phone number
- Email address
- Website

This will make it easy for people to get in touch with you and learn more about your services. Be sure to include your professional designation, such as "Realtor" or "Broker," to showcase your expertise and credibility.

Another benefit of professional business cards is that they can help you build relationships with potential clients. By handing out your business card, you are making it easy for them to contact you later, increasing your chances of closing a sale.

When you include your photo on your business card, you make it more personal and memorable. Which will help build trust and establish a connection with potential clients.

It's also important to ensure that your business cards exude professionalism. This can be achieved using high-quality paper, a clean and modern design, and professional-looking fonts. Additionally, by including a professional headshot or photo of a property, you can make your business card more visually appealing and memorable.

When designing your business card, keep it simple, clean, and easy to read. The less cluttered your card is, the more professional it looks. Avoid using more than one or two colors, and stick to a consistent design. Avoid too many graphics or too much text, and stick to the most important information.

It's also important to ensure that all of the contact information on your business card is up-to-date and correct. This may seem like a small detail, but it's important to ensure that potential clients can reach you easily. Make sure to check and update your business cards at least once a year or when you have any changes in your contact information.

## 93. CHECK OUT EXPIRED LISTINGS

Expired listings are a valuable source of potential new leads for realtors. These listings are properties that were previously on the market but did not sell and were taken off by their owner. While some realtors may overlook expired listings as a source of new business, they can be a great opportunity to find new leads and grow your business.

One of the main benefits of working with expired listings is that they represent a motivated seller. These sellers are typically more willing to negotiate. They may be more open to working with a realtor to get their property sold. Additionally, by working with expired listings, you can demonstrate your expertise and knowledge of the local market, which can help you build trust and establish a connection with the seller.

Another benefit of working with expired listings is that they can be a great source of new leads. By reaching out to the owners of expired listings, you can offer your services and show them how you can help them sell their property. Networking with other realtors in your area is a great way to learn about newly expired listings. Learning about these listings as soon as they become available gives you a head start over your competition.

It's also important to understand why the property didn't sell when it was previously on the market. This can be achieved by researching the property's history and contacting the previous agent. Often, the reason for the property not selling can be due to overpricing, poor marketing, or lack of attention from the agent. By identifying and addressing the problem, you can increase your chances of successfully selling the property.

When working with expired listings, it's important to be persistent and professional. By following up with the seller regularly and providing them with valuable information about the market and other properties, you can demonstrate your commitment to helping them sell their property.

By providing them with a marketing plan and a list of things you will do to help them sell their property, you can show them that you are the right person for the job.

## 94. DISTRIBUTE DOOR HANGERS FOR EFFECTIVE DOOR TO DOOR MARKETING

Door-to-door marketing, also known as door-hanger marketing, is a cost-effective and targeted way for realtors to reach potential clients in their local area. By physically distributing door hangers, realtors can introduce themselves to new potential clients by physically distributing door hangers and promote their services personally and directly.

One of the main benefits of door-to-door marketing is that it allows realtors to target specific neighborhoods. Realtors can reach potential clients who are most likely to be interested in their services by focusing on a specific area. Additionally, door-to-door marketing allows realtors to reach potential clients who may not be actively looking for a realtor but could benefit from their services.

Another benefit of door-to-door marketing is that it allows realtors to stand out from their competition. By physically distributing door hangers, realtors can introduce themselves to potential clients personally and directly, which can help them build trust and establish a connection. Additionally, door-to-door marketing allows realtors to provide potential clients with information about their services and qualifications, which can help them stand out from other realtors in the area.

When creating door hangers for door-to-door marketing, it's important to ensure they are professional, clear, and easy to read. The design should be simple and include your contact information, a picture of yourself, and a short message about your services. Also, consider including a call-to-action, such as a promotion or a special offer, which can encourage potential clients to contact you.

It's also important to respect people's privacy when conducting door-to-door marketing. Always knock on the door or ring the bell before leaving a door hanger, and be mindful of the time of day you are doing the marketing and the neighborhood you are in. Follow the guidelines of your local municipality or community regarding door-to-door marketing.

Finally, door-to-door marketing is not just about distributing door hangers; it's also about following up. Keep track of the door hangers you distribute and follow up with the potential clients you meet. By following up, you can connect with potential clients and increase your chances of closing a sale.

# PEOPLE-BASED
# MARKETING IDEAS

## 95. ALWAYS CALL AFTER A HOUSE VISIT

One of the most important marketing strategies for realtors is to always call after a house visit. This simple step can help you build relationships with potential clients and generate more leads.

When potential buyers visit a property, they are usually interested in it and consider making an offer. You can answer any questions by following up with them after the visit. They may have questions about the property or the buying process, and provide them with any additional information they may need. This can help you establish yourself as a trusted advisor and make it more likely that they will come to you when they are ready to buy or sell a property.

When we follow up with potential buyers after a house visit, you can also get a sense of their level of interest in the property and whether or not they are likely to make an offer. This can help you prioritize your follow-up efforts and focus on the most promising leads.

Another benefit of calling after a house visit is that it helps you stay top of mind with potential clients. By regularly reaching out to them, you can ensure that they remember you and your services when they are ready to buy or sell a property.

Lastly, always calling after a house visit can also help you build relationships with other realtors in the area. Stay in touch with other agents. You can learn about new listings and potential buyers before they hit the market and collaborate with other agents to find the right property for your clients.

Calling after a house visit is an effective marketing strategy for realtors. It can help you build relationships with potential clients, generate more leads, stay top of mind and collaborate with other agents in the area. By taking the time to call after a house visit, you can increase your chances of making a sale and establish yourself as a trusted and professional agent.

## 96. CONTINUE TO HELP EVEN AFTER THE SALE

As a realtor, your job is to help people buy and sell properties. But your work doesn't have to end once the sale is complete. By continuing to help your clients even after the sale, you can build lasting relationships and establish yourself as a trusted advisor in the industry.

Here are some ways you can continue to help your clients even after the sale:

1. **Provide Moving Resources:** After the sale is complete, your clients will be in the process of moving into their new home. Provide them with resources such as a list of recommended movers, storage facilities, and packing tips to make the transition as smooth as possible.
2. **Help with Home Improvement:** Your clients may have a list of home improvement projects they want to tackle in their new home. Provide them with resources such as a list of local contractors, architects, and home improvement stores to help them get started.
3. **Offer Maintenance Tips**: A new home can be overwhelming. Offer your clients tips on maintaining their new home, such as regular cleaning and maintenance schedules.
4. **Connect Them With Local Services:** Your clients will need to connect with local services such as utilities, cable, and internet providers. Provide them with a list of local providers and contact information to make this process as easy as possible.

160

5. **Keep in Touch:** After the sale is complete, it's important to keep in touch with your clients. Send them occasional updates on the local real estate market, and let them know you're available to help if they need anything.

By continuing to help your clients even after the sale, you'll build trust and establish yourself as a valuable resource in the industry. Your clients will appreciate the extra effort you put in to make their transition into their new home as smooth as possible. They'll be more likely to refer their friends and family to you.

As a realtor, your job is not just to help people buy and sell properties and to be a valuable resource in their journey of owning a new home. Your client's satisfaction should be your main goal. Provide them with resources and tips, and be available to help them even after the sale. This is a great way to achieve client satisfaction. Remember, happy clients can become your best referrals in the future.

## 97. DON'T FORGET YOUR FORMER CLIENTS

As a realtor, it's important to remember that your former clients are valuable assets to your business. Not only can they provide you with valuable referrals, but they may also be in the market to buy or sell again in the future.

Here are some ways you can stay in touch with your former clients and remind them of your services:

1. **Send a Follow-up Letter:** After the sale is complete, send your clients a follow-up letter thanking them for their business. Remind them that you can help them with any future real estate needs.

2. **Stay in Touch via Email or Social Media**: Keep your clients updated on the local real estate market. Inform them about any new listings or open houses that may interest them.

3. **Send a Personalized Card:** Send your former clients a personalized card on special occasions such as anniversaries or birthdays.

4. **Offer a Referral Program:** Encourage your former clients to refer their friends and family to you by offering them a referral fee or a gift card.

5. **Host an Event:** Host an event such as an open house or a client appreciation party and invite your former clients. This will allow them to see you in action and remind them of your services.

By staying in touch with your former clients, you'll be top of mind when they're ready to buy or sell again. Showing them that you value their business and are still available to help will make them feel appreciated. Making them more likely to refer their friends and family to you. Remember, your former clients can become your best advocates for your business, and keeping that relationship strong is essential.

It's important to remember that your former clients are valuable assets to your business.

Below are a few ways to stay in touch:

- Offering them a referral program.
- Hosting an event.
- Sending personalized cards.

These are great ways to remind them of your services and to be top of mind when they're ready to buy or sell again.

Remember that your former clients can become your best advocates for your business, and keeping that relationship strong is essential.

## 98. STANDING OUT IN A SEA OF SUITS WITH A FUNNY T-SHIRT OR HOODIE

As a realtor, standing out in a sea of competition is important. One unique and effective way to do this is by incorporating a funny t-shirt or hoodie into your marketing strategy.

Here's how:

1.  **Wear it to Open Houses:** Open houses are a great opportunity to showcase your personality and connect with potential clients. Wearing a funny t-shirt or hoodie can make you more approachable and memorable and serve as a conversation starter.
2.  **Use it in Social Media Posts:** Social media is a powerful tool for realtors. Incorporating a funny t-shirt or hoodie into your posts can help you stand out. Use it in photos or videos of you at listings, open houses, or even in your daily life.
3.  **Give it Away as a Prize:** Host a contest on social media or at an open house. Offering a funny t-shirt or hoodie as a prize can be a great way to generate engagement and attract new clients.
4.  **Wear it to Networking Events:** Networking events are a great way to connect with other realtors and potential clients. Wearing a funny t-shirt or hoodie can help you stand out and make a lasting impression.

5. **Use it in Your Marketing Materials:** Incorporate a photo of yourself wearing a funny t-shirt or hoodie into your marketing materials, such as business cards or brochures. Helping you stand out and make a memorable impression.

By incorporating a funny t-shirt or hoodie into your marketing strategy, you can showcase your personality, stand out in a sea of competition, and attract new clients. Remember to keep it tasteful and professional, and choose a shirt or hoodie that reflects your unique style and personality.

As a realtor, it's important to stand out from the competition and make a lasting impression on potential clients. Using a funny t-shirt or hoodie can be a unique and effective way to showcase your personality and connect with potential clients.

What can you do with it?

- Wear it to open houses.
- Use it in social media posts.
- Give it away as a prize.
- Attend networking events.
- Use it in your marketing materials.

Remember, keep it tasteful and professional, and choose a shirt or hoodie that reflects your unique style and personality.

## 99. ALWAYS USE PROFESSIONAL PHOTOS

Photos play a crucial role in showcasing your listings and attracting potential buyers. They are often the first thing that a buyer sees when browsing listings, and they can make or break their decision to schedule a viewing. Therefore, putting effort and thought into the photos you use to represent your listings is essential.

Hiring a professional photographer is one way to ensure that your photos are top-notch. A professional can capture the best angles and lighting of the property, making it look its best. They can also help to stage the property, making it more appealing to potential buyers. However, suppose you don't have the budget to hire a professional. In that case, you can still take great photos by following some basic photography tips.

**First,** make sure that the photos are taken in good lighting. Natural light is best, so try to take photos during the daytime or early evening when the sun is shining. This will help to bring out the color and detail of the property.

**Second,** take wide-angle shots that show the entire room or space. This will give buyers a sense of the layout and flow of the property. Also, take close-ups of any unique features, such as built-in bookshelves or a fireplace. This will give buyers a sense of the property's quality and attention to detail.

**Third,** clean and declutter the property before taking photos. This will make the property look more spacious and inviting. It's a good idea to remove any personal items, such as family photos or artwork. Friendly reminder; put down those toilet seats! Nothing ruins a photo like a toilet.

Use them strategically. For example, you can use photos on your website and social media to generate interest in a property before it's even listed. You can also use them in brochures and flyers to give buyers a sense of what the property looks like before they even schedule a viewing.

Photos are essential for any realtor looking to showcase their listings and attract potential buyers. Investing in high-quality photos and using them strategically can give your listings the edge they need to stand out in a crowded market.

## 100.GENERATING LEADS WITH FLYERS, POSTCARDS, AND BROCHURES

Flyers, postcards, and brochures have been used as marketing tools in the real estate industry for many years. Some may argue that these traditional marketing methods in today's digital age may be considered outdated. However, there are several reasons why these tools are still effective for generating leads for realtors.

**First**, these materials provide a tangible and physical representation of the property. Potential clients can hold the flyer, postcard, or brochure in their hands and take the time to examine it at their leisure. This can be especially effective when generating leads for high-end properties, where visuals are crucial to showcase the property's features and attributes.

**Second,** these materials can be targeted to specific areas or neighborhoods. For example, postcards can be sent to specific neighborhoods where potential clients are likely to be interested in buying or selling a property. This targeted approach can be more effective than a general mass mailing campaign.

**Third**, these materials can be used in a variety of ways. For example, flyers can be distributed door-to-door or at local events. Postcards can be sent through the mail, and brochures can be left at open houses or given to potential clients during one-on-one meetings. This versatility allows realtors to use these materials in the most effective way for their specific needs.

Using these materials allows realtors to establish themselves as experts in a specific area or neighborhood. By providing detailed information about the local market and the properties in the area, realtors can position themselves as valuable resources for potential clients. This can help to build trust and establish a personal connection with potential clients.

Furthermore, these materials can also be used to create a sense of exclusivity and urgency. By promoting a new listing or an upcoming open house, realtors can create a sense of excitement and encourage potential clients to take action.

While digital marketing strategies can be effective, flyers, postcards, and brochures are still valuable tools for generating leads in the real estate industry. They provide a tangible and physical representation of the property, can be targeted to specific areas or neighborhoods, and can be used in various ways. Additionally, SoldOutHouses.com's Pro Membership program offers a wide range of templates and resources to help real estate professionals create professional-looking materials.

## BONUS IDEA - TAKE ADVANTAGE OF POWERFUL MARKETING TOOLS.

Real estate marketing can be challenging, especially in today's digital age. Finding the right tools and strategies to generate leads and close sales can be time-consuming and costly. However, there is a solution that can help real estate professionals succeed in their industry - **SoldOutHouses.com's Pro Membership Program.**

I started SoldOutHouses.com as an ex-real estate agent. I understand the difficulties and struggles that come with real estate marketing. I wanted to create a website that provides real estate professionals with the tools and resources they need to succeed in the industry. And with SoldOutHouses.com's Pro Membership program, real estate professionals can access all the real estate marketing templates they need to succeed in their industry.

The Pro Membership program offers a wide range of real estate marketing templates and resources, including done-for-you content that is ready to use. This includes over 1700 templates, social media posts, articles, swipe files, funnels, and even offline materials such as letters and open house signs.

This membership gives real estate professionals everything they need to generate more leads, close more sales, and drive more traffic online and offline.

I started this website to provide a solution for real estate professionals struggling with real estate marketing and make their lives easier. And I believe that with the right tools and resources, it is possible to succeed in the industry.

SoldOutHouses.com's Pro Membership Program offers a wide range of real estate marketing templates and resources. These tools help real estate professionals generate more leads, close more sales, and drive more traffic.

If you're looking for a way to take your real estate marketing to the next level, consider trying the Pro Membership program on SoldOutHouses.com at https://soldouthouses.com/pro/ today.

# AN EPILOGUE

Congratulations on completing this book! By now, you should have a solid understanding of how you can generate leads and boost sales as a realtor. From social media marketing to website optimization, content marketing, and offline marketing, countless opportunities exist to reach and connect with potential clients.

It is important to remember that to be successful in the digital landscape, you need to be consistent and creative and stay up to date with the latest trends. Also, it's crucial to have a clear target audience, understand their needs and tailor your marketing strategies accordingly.

Keep in mind that there is no one-size-fits-all approach to real estate marketing. Finding the right mix of strategies and tactics that work for you and your business will take some experimentation and tweaking. But with the right tools and techniques, you can succeed and turn your real estate business into a thriving enterprise.

Lastly, I would like to remind you that this book is only a starting point. There is much more to learn and explore in digital marketing. I encourage you to keep learning and experimenting with new strategies and tactics.

Once again, if you're looking for additional resources and real estate marketing tools and templates, visit

https://SoldOutHouses.com, and follow our YouTube channel at https://youtube.com/@soldouthouses.

Thank you for reading, and best of luck in your real estate marketing efforts!

# RESOURCES

Thanks for taking this book; the following are some resources that can help you take your real estate business to the next level.

**1. The Ultimate Real Estate Marketing Checklist (Free)**

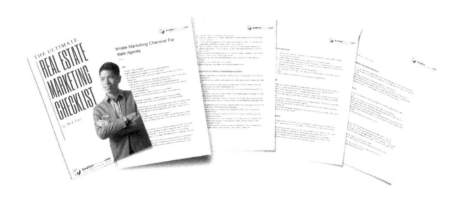

Get 86 proven real estate marketing ideas
to generate more leads online.

Please go to https://soldouthouses.com/checklist
to download your free checklist.

## 2. Sold Out Houses Pro Membership

You can also join our pro membership to get access to over 1700+ real estate marketing tools & templates for only a few bucks a day.

Go to https://soldouthouses.com/pro/
to learn more about this special package.

### 3. Our Digital Marketing Services

Want my team to take care of your internet marketing for you?

Visit Our site at https://services.soldouthouses.com/ to see what you can do to bring your real estate marketing to the next level.

### 4. 150 done-for-you real estate infographics

Get your social media content ready in the next few minutes.

You can get your infographic package at
https://soldouthouses.com/infographics.

## 5. 360 real estate social media post templates

Create professional social media content
quickly with those templates

You can get those templates at
https://soldouthouses.com/socialmediaposttemplates

## 6.360 real estate ad templates

Create professional social media ad images
quickly with these templates.

You can get all templates at
https://soldouthouses.com/adtemplates

## 7. Easy Real Estate Funnels
## (Done-for-you website & funnel templates)

Want to have a professional real estate website? Get our done-for-you website and funnel template and get your website up and running quickly.

Learn more at
https://soldouthouses.com/easyfunnel

## 8 10X Leadgen Masterclass

Discover how to generate more leads with digital marketing.

Sign up here at

https://soldouthouses.com/masterclass

Printed in the USA
CPSIA information can be obtained
at www.ICGtesting.com
LVHW011804030224
770871LV00003B/496